RAISING T

RICHMOND METHODIST CHURCH

RICHMOND METHODIST CHURCH

RAISING THE DEAD

*The Art of the Preacher
as Public Performer*

Colin Morris

RICHMOND METHODIST CHURCH

Fount
An Imprint of HarperCollinsPublishers

Fount Paperbacks is an Imprint of
HarperCollins*Religious*
Part of HarperCollins*Publishers*
77–85 Fulham Palace Road, London W6 8JB

First published in Great Britain
in 1996 by Fount Paperbacks

1 3 5 7 9 10 8 6 4 2

Copyright © 1996 Colin Morris

Colin Morris asserts the moral right to be
identified as the author of this work

A catalogue record for this book is
available from the British Library

0 00 627991 0

Printed and bound in Great Britain by
HarperCollinsManufacturing Glasgow

CONDITIONS OF SALE
This book is sold subject to the condition that it
shall not, by way of trade or otherwise, be lent, re-sold,
hired out or otherwise circulated without the publisher's
prior consent in any form of binding or cover other
than that in which it is published and without a
similar condition including this condition being
imposed on the subsequent purchaser.

All rights reserved. No part of this publication may be
reproduced, stored in a retrieval system, or transmitted,
in any form or by any means, electronic, mechanical,
photocopying, recording or otherwise, without the prior
permission of the publishers.

For Paul Hulme and the people of Wesley's Chapel, City Road, London – guardians of Wesley's pulpit.

Preaching is thirty minutes in which to raise the dead

John Ruskin

CONTENTS

THREE: THE PERFORMANCE

INTRODUCTION

'DON'T SHOOT THE PREACHER'

They tell us that the day of preaching is over, mortally wounded by popular entertainment and finished off by television. Mind you, they've been telling us this for decades. Preaching has been under sentence of death for the whole of my ministry; indeed, much further back than that. When the Lyman-Beecher Lectures on Preaching at Yale were established in the 1870s, the final lecture of the first series was headed, 'Is Preaching Finished?' The lecturer answered with a resounding 'No!', but the fact that the question was even thought worth asking in high Victorian times is significant. A decade later, A. B. Davidson, the great Scottish Hebrew scholar who was also one of the most sought-after preachers of his day, complained, 'Preaching is at a very low ebb and unless something is done urgently to rectify matters I fear for the future of the Church of God.'[1] And in 1949, another great preacher, W. E. Sangster, began his book on sermon construction with the words, 'Preaching is in the shadows ...'[2]

Yet as a matter of crude statistics, this coming Sunday hundreds of thousands of sermons will be preached from pulpits in Britain; many millions throughout the world. They may be good, bad or indifferent, but they will happen. And in spite of decades of experimentation with drama, dance, dialogue, over-the-garden-wall type chats and twin-pulpit debates, the honest-to-God sermon still bears the main weight of Christian discourse. And in a form that has remained remarkably consistent over the centuries.

In fact, the modern preacher is the lineal descendant of the Preaching Friars of the thirteenth century. It was they who evolved the notion of the sermon as an argument with a logical structure using illustrations to make their points. At a time when most clergy felt that all they were required to do was celebrate the Mass, the Preaching Friars not only elevated the sermon in the divine office but dared to claim that if it was a straight choice, preaching came first. As St Bernardino of Siena put it, 'If of these two things you can do only one, either hear the Mass or hear the sermon, you should let the Mass go rather than the sermon for there is less peril in not hearing the Mass than in not hearing the sermon.'[3]

But let's not dwell on the past. Because these are tough times for the Church, nostalgia sometimes tempts us to look back to a Golden Age in the past when the pews were packed week by week and giants stalked our pulpits holding vast congregations enraptured by their oratory. Certainly, when the Church was numerically stronger there *were* giants who commanded great congregations, but away from the Himalayan peaks, hidden in the foothills, were also thousands of preachers addressing the proverbial baker's dozen.

A recent book puts all this in perspective. It is called *The Myth of the Empty Church* by Robin Gill.[4] The author demonstrates by the use of population census figures that the Church's folk-memory is indeed fallible. Since the Industrial Revolution, Britain has been a society with far too many churches and chapels for the available population to fill. And when a pulpit star built up his congregation, it was often though not always at the expense of other congregations in the vicinity rather than by attracting the non-churched masses.

What has undoubtedly been undermined is the notion of preaching as public entertainment. In Victorian times the crowds queued to hear C. H. Spurgeon, Joseph Parker or Alexander Whyte as they would today outside a West End theatre or Wembley Stadium to attend a show. These were great men of God but they were also virtuoso performers whose sermons were vastly enjoyed and discussed afterwards as we might comment on a television programme or a football match. Spurgeon's Sunday sermons were in fact carried by Monday's newspapers on both sides of the Atlantic. Now there is a vast entertainment industry to meet that particular need, so the trade of preaching as a diversion for the masses has not just declined but vanished.

But even then the preaching megastars were a rare breed. The Church has not been borne on the wings of stirring oratory by pulpit Titans but carried painfully along on the backs of journeyman-preachers, lay and ministerial. The bench-mark standard of preaching has never been that set by the likes of Spurgeon, Parker, Weatherhead or Sangster in addressing vast congregations; they were always the glorious exceptions, as are geniuses in any field. The standard is and always has been the preacher of modest attainments faithfully ministering the Word of God to unexceptional numbers of Christians. If the evidence for what some call the parlous state of preaching is the modest number who gather to hear the average preacher then when has preaching not been on the way out? This is no cause for complacency but at least challenges the notion that there is a kind of Messianic Secret of preaching known to our forebears which we have lost.

Granted, the size of the average congregation has, with some happy exceptions, sharply declined over past decades and left the preacher painfully exposed – to the extent that there ought to be attached to our pulpits a notice like that hanging over the piano in the saloons of the Wild West, 'Don't Shoot the Pianist, He's Doing His Best'. Don't shoot the preacher because the church is half empty. There *is* a tendency in the modern Church to blame shrinking numbers on poor preaching as simple cause and effect. This grievous injustice not only undermines the preacher's morale but also distorts the Church's thinking about mission.

To use Dr Sangster's phrase, even were preaching to come out of the shadows, there is no guarantee that congregational numbers would inevitably grow. The Church's numerical decline is a complex phenomenon and it is unlikely that a change in any single factor will reverse it. Indeed, the only thing that can is the mysterious operation of the Holy Spirit, whose presence cannot be commanded, predicted or legislated for. In the meantime, the Church's task according to our liturgy is to proclaim the Lord's death till he come. And it is reasonable to assume that any improvement in the standard of preaching must enable the congregations that *are* there, together with the preacher, to accomplish what the man or woman in the pulpit cannot achieve alone – lift a church out of the doldrums and energize it for mission.

Hence, the preacher has no monopoly of the task which Leslie Weatherhead was fond of summarizing as making God real and changing the lives of men and women. For though preaching is in one sense a solo performance – and there's no getting away from that – in another, it is a liturgical act, a central enterprise of the whole Church of God.

The living word issues from a living community. As Paul wrote, the manifold wisdom of God is made known through the *Church* – which presumably includes individual pulpit geniuses but also many Christians who couldn't string two words together in public to save their lives. The preacher speaks but it is the Church which preaches.

Preachers may occasionally feel like Sisyphus eternally condemned to push a great stone uphill, but God has not cast them in the role of Atlas doomed to carry the whole world on their backs, for they are but one facet of that many splendoured thing, the liturgical, sacramental and pastoral life of the community of faith. And the most powerful expression of the Gospel is still the witness of individual Christians who preach mute but magnificent sermons by bearing about in their bodies the dying of the Lord Jesus.

Yet if we want to hang on to the Church, we must keep at the business of preaching and trust the promises of God concerning it in the teeth of the sceptics and woe-sayers. We have passed this way before and will again, for the Church's story has not been a triumphal progression from glory to glory but a contorted, cyclic thing – long slow ends and sudden beginnings, decay and renewal, death and resurrection. In every age we find ourselves having to fight over the same ground we thought had been secured by previous generations of believers. Reaffirming the centrality of preaching is one such never-ending task.

This book began life as a series of letters to a young solicitor called Andrea who had just begun to preach and asked me for advice – I have kept the personal form of address. These letters were afterwards published in the *Methodist Recorder*, and I'm grateful to the Editor,

Michael Taylor, for permission to reproduce material I used there. The articles sparked off a huge correspondence about preaching from which I received as much as I gave, and I'm grateful to all the preachers, clerical and lay, who shared their experiences with me.

I've not concerned myself overmuch with the sheer nuts and bolts of preaching – voice production, detailed attention to sermon beginnings, conclusions and illustrations and the like. Of course, they are vital, but I'm sure they are best taught face to face, either by tutors or in sermon classes. But I do believe the issues I raise are central to any real understanding of what preaching is and is not, what makes a sermon good, bad or indifferent and what motivates the preacher as a public performer.

Ruskin's definition of the sermon from which this book's title is taken is awesome in its expectations. In honesty, not many erstwhile corpses stride out of churches, bursting with new life as a consequence of the spiritual kiss-of-life administered from the pulpit between the third and fourth hymns. Latter-day Lazaruses who emerge from the tomb blinking in the sunlight in response to a command that could not be disobeyed are thin on the ground, but the miracle does happen, so however inadequate we may feel, we must stick to our task because as Paul put it, 'God resolved to save believers by the sheer folly of preaching.'

ONE

THE PREACHER

PREACH – IF YOU MUST!

So you've been given a licence to preach. Congratulations. But treat it more like a firearms certificate than a fishing licence. Dangling a rod and line in the water is a pleasant enough pastime and will do little harm, except to the odd fish. A loaded firearm is a different matter; in the hands of the wicked, the careless or the deranged it can cause mayhem. Well, a note to preach has its dangers too. For preachers preach not only at their own souls' peril, which is risky enough, but to the peril of their hearers' souls, which is even worse.

'No one deserves the wrath of God more than the preacher', wrote the theologian Karl Barth in the course of a magnificent rant about the sheer impertinence of preaching, 'What are you doing with the Word of God on your lips? ... Upon what grounds do you assume the role of mediator between heaven and earth? ... Do you with impunity usurp prerogatives of God?'[5] Barth goes on and on hurling one contemptuous bolt after another at the hapless preacher to the point where one concludes, 'Well, if this is what God thinks about his messengers, no wonder there are so many gaps in our preaching schedules.'

It's not hard to understand why Moses, Isaiah, Ezekiel,

Jonah and many another hero of the faith begged without success to be excused from the office of divine messenger – 'I am a man of unclean lips ... I am but a youth ... I'm a simple herdsman ... I have an urgent engagement in Tarshish.' Pardon my presumption in referring to myself in such illustrious company but had I read that passage from Karl Barth forty years ago, I might indeed have exchanged my note to preach for a fishing licence. At least the fresh air would do me good.

Hence, to balance my congratulations I offer you sympathy. It's not that the task you've embarked upon is difficult; it isn't, it's strictly impossible. It will entrance, infuriate, depress and exhilarate you, but if as a preacher you ever reach the point through vast experience that it becomes a doddle, it doesn't mean you have mastered the art of preaching but that pride has mastered you.

It would be understandable were you to feel that a newcomer to the pulpit deserves encouragement rather than doom-laden warnings. After all, if we hope for successors, preachers of my generation would be wise to proclaim the satisfactions of the preacher's vocation in big letters and confine its perils to the small print. I respectfully disagree. Better by far that some of the Church's pulpits should be empty each Sunday as a mute testimony to the ineffable glory of God than that they should be filled with cheery prattlers who don't know the difference between holy wisdom and verbal fog.

One shrewd minister I much respected always advised those who announced they felt called to enter the ordained ministry, 'For God's sake, don't! Not if you can possibly stay out!' In the same spirit, I would say to you, 'Preach, if you must!' For as that lion of the pulpit Dr Alexander Whyte once told a young minister who was almost incoherent with enthusiasm about the excitement and drama of preaching, 'Aye, but it's a long sore fight to the end.'[6]

The cellist Pablo Casals was once climbing in America when a loose rock crashed down and fractured one of his fingers. His companions were appalled but when he looked down at his mangled finger his first reaction was, 'Thank God, I'll never have to play the cello again!' and added, 'Dedication to one's art does involve a form of enslavement.'[7] Pablo Casals' comment will probably strike a chord with many experienced preachers for whom preaching is both a privilege and a burden, a form of enslavement to a task whose goal remains for ever out of reach.

Little wonder St Cyprian confessed that he would rather say a hundred Masses than preach one sermon or that Martin Luther wrote, 'Although I am old and experienced in speaking, I tremble whenever I ascend the pulpit.' And one preacher of whom it could be justly claimed that he possessed genius, the Victorian F. W. Robertson of Brighton, said after a bad Sunday, 'I wish I didn't hate preaching so much.'[8] Many less eminent preachers will confess they approach the pulpit with an inevitable sense of impending failure, and those generous members of the congregation at the church door who afterwards express gratitude for an excellent sermon usually make them feel worse. I must qualify that. Occasionally after a service I have been thanked by someone for a sermon I didn't actually preach but he or she heard. One can only conclude that the Holy Spirit got through in spite of me.

Preaching can be such a torment that I do not trivialize the words of Jesus in claiming that the preacher entering the pulpit is entitled to cry, 'I have a baptism to undergo and what constraint I am under until the ordeal is over.'

And yet ... the preacher is driven there, in some sense possessed. The prophet Jeremiah confessed that when he was not preaching God's word it was like a fire trapped inside him burning him up.

Jeremiah said another interesting thing about his call to God's service. He used an image the translators of the King James Version found a little strong for their taste so they substituted the English word 'deceived' for the Hebrew word 'seduced'. His declaration should have read, 'O Lord, you have seduced me, and I was seduced; you are stronger than I am and prevailed.'⁹ To put it plainly, he is saying that he was swept off his feet and ravished. He was press-ganged, not simply chosen but overwhelmed.

And though a divine call is the decisive thing in every true decision to become a preacher, there is also an element of human compulsion, even addiction, in it. The preacher is attracted to the pulpit as an alcoholic to the bottle or a gambler to the betting shop. This demon may not yet be a roaring passion in you; possibly just the beginnings of a persistent itch, but without it there can be no inspired preaching.

So I hope you will get intelligent delight out of preaching and feel that natural buzz compounded of dread and fascination whenever you first catch sight of a congregation. Actually, it's not entirely a natural buzz; one element in it is quite supernatural – awe at the possibility that through you God might choose to work a miracle in the life of someone who will hear you.

NO CARBON COPIES

When asked for advice about preaching, I am reluctant to offer any, not through mock-modesty but because

4

preaching is such a mysterious and individual thing that in my experience those who take too much notice of the style of others are in danger of missing the whole point of it.

The college at which I studied as a theological student divided up roughly into Soperians and Sangsterians, modelled on those two Methodist pulpit giants, Doctors Soper and Sangster who for decades packed huge London churches. The Soperians affected smart grey suits and red ties and shared the socialism and pacifism of the great man. The Sangsterians were sombre-suited, winsome in pulpit voice and had little silver hammers that split any biblical text into three neat points for preaching purposes.

We students learned much by studying the technique of these outstanding preachers but the more sensible of us realized the pointlessness of slavish imitation – which is acting, not preaching. There is a place for the mimic but it isn't in the pulpit. One of the old rabbis said that God never does the same thing twice. However long history wears on, never again will another W. E. Sangster or Donald Soper grace the pulpit. Nor will the Church be blessed by that exact combination of personal strengths or weaknesses you can bring to bear on the task of preaching. So don't try to obliterate your individuality; it's the only truly original gift you have to offer – everything else to do with preaching has been said and done a million times before in Christian history.

God's dealings with the world are mysterious and the only firm evidence we have of him acting directly in human affairs is through the agency of personal encounter. I suppose he might have entrusted the Gospel to angels as his messengers; they no doubt would convey the truth with greater accuracy and cause the kind of stir advertising agencies seek when they want to grab the public's attention. My theological dictionary defines angels as 'simply messengers;

their nature is of no significance'. In that case, the preacher is certainly no angel because his or her nature is of *supreme* significance, for the Gospel does not exist in a vacuum; it is fashioned out of the preacher's qualities both distinctive and shared.

Even our human frailties are an essential part of the preaching process. It's not just when we are at our best in the pulpit, fluent, competent, on top of our theme, that God speaks through us. He is also making a point when we are reduced to stammering inadequacy, totally unable to match up the magnitude of the task we have foolishly taken on. The Authorized Version mistranslates 1 Corinthians 1:21 as 'the foolishness of preaching'. What Paul meant is that it is the Gospel itself and not our presentation of it that is both foolish and yet wiser than human wit.

Let the error stand. At least when we make idiots of ourselves in public and appear like small children slopping around in our father's shoes, apparently playing at a game which is completely beyond us, we are ironically testifying to the glory of the Gospel. We have failed in the past and are certain to come a cropper again, but the fact that like battered pugilists we are prepared to get back into the ring for another go at least suggests there is urgency in what we are struggling to do.

Study closely the account in the book of Genesis (chapter 32) of Jacob wrestling all night with an unknown adversary by the ford at the River Jabbok. One tradition identifies the stranger as an angel; another suggests Jacob's adversary is God himself in human form – whichever: his opponent is the embodiment of divine communication. By the time the sun rises and Jacob's adversary leaves him, several things have happened. He has a fresh sense of his own identity, he believes he's been wrestling with God though he isn't quite sure, and he's been crippled in the struggle.

That story says something fundamental about the personal nature of all communication, and supremely about preaching. Communication is the encounter between personalities who whatever they gain by way of information in the process discover more about each other. There is all the difference in the world between conveying information to people and communicating with them. We *inform* when we pass on bits of knowledge; we *communicate* when we disclose something of ourselves in the act of passing on the bits of knowledge.

Communication is a costly business. As a legacy of his encounter with God, Jacob comes away with a pronounced limp. It's as though God were saying, 'By all means meet me in mutual self-disclosure, but only if you are prepared to pay the price.' It was not a Socratic dialogue but a wrestling match Jacob was forced to take part in – a thing of blood and sweat and bruises. This means that a congregation is entitled to detect the blood-streak of personal experience in all we say. We do not stand in the pulpit immaculate and unmarked but metaphorically black-and-blue from our private jousting with God.

Ralph Waldo Emerson describes how he went to hear a preacher who, he said, sorely tempted him to quit the Church. 'He had not one word intimating that he had laughed or wept, was married or in love, had been commended or cheated, or vexed. If he had ever lived or acted, we were not the wiser for it. The capital secret of his profession, namely, to convert life into truth, he had not learned.'[10] 'Converting life into truth' – could there be a more succinct way of describing the preaching process?

We are taught that the validity of the sacrament of Holy Communion does not in the end depend upon the personality of the officiating priest or minister. One can't make the same claim about the sacrament of the Word. It is not enough to mount the pulpit steps out of a general belief that the Gospel is true; it must be true for you, otherwise you are just a person speaking about religion rather than a religious person speaking – and the one place where you ought never to speak *about* religion is the pulpit.

Religion is not a spectator sport, though a surprising number of people treat it as though it were. It is quite possible to talk about religion as a fascinating subject without having had any personal exposure to it, which is a little like studying underwater life by watching it through the window of a diving bell. You can't really understand the inner dynamics of what's going on without getting into the water and sharing the fascination and dangers of the environment.

One could construct a spiritual biography of many of the great preachers simply by analysing their sermons. The nineteenth-century American preacher, Bishop William Quayle, said, 'Preaching is not the art of making a sermon and delivering it; it is the art of making a preacher and delivering that.'[11] It is the latest report from the front on what God has been doing in the preacher's life and in the life of the world. To put it another way, what is in the sermon must be in the preacher first.

This is a sceptical age which distrusts all formal authority. We preachers are required to lay our integrity on the line with complete openness. We cannot hide behind the skirts of the bishops or the robes of the doctors. We cannot pick other people's flowers, deliver other people's sermons or recite other people's beliefs with any hope of carrying conviction. In one sense, we have not been sent from God with a message, we *are* that message, its weight is our weight and its convincing power is in direct proportion to our spiritual and intellectual capacity to open ourselves to the Gospel.

There is an art gallery in Rome which houses a collection of busts of the Roman Emperors, from the earliest to the last, each one done by a sculptor who was a contemporary of the particular Caesar portrayed. It is possible to trace the decay of a great art from the magnificent Greek marbles of the earliest emperors to the crude representations, little more than wooden dolls, of their Gothic successors. The explanation is simple. The later sculptors were so overawed by their giant predecessors that they slavishly copied their style rather than modelling from the living subject.[12]

What goes for sculpture applies also to preaching. The preacher must model from the living subject, not copy the work of the masters. Slavish imitation of our betters saps the springs of our creativity; a genuine if modest original becomes a large-scale counterfeit. Our motives may be honourable because we want to offer God the very best of which we are capable, but it is a mistake to imagine that he prefers our echo of someone else's Te Deum to our own original praise.

So never suppress the essential you because of some mistaken notion that you'd be a better preacher if you were to model yourself on one of your heroes or ideals. God doesn't work through carbon copies; only originals. I too have my pulpit heroes but I know that when I have to give an account of my stewardship, God won't say, 'Why weren't you Reinhold Niebuhr or Leslie Weatherhead or George MacLeod?' He'll say, 'Why weren't you Colin Morris?'

And yet ... here is a paradox. The preacher having asserted his or her individuality must then forget, even transcend it. If we are thinking about natural aptitudes and skills, then indeed we must be ourselves and not yield to the temptation of being pale imitations of others. But morally and spiritually, we must be prepared, as John the Baptist said, to decrease in order that Christ may increase. Paul put it in a terse paradox, 'I, yet not I.'

How is this done? What can deliver the preacher from the twin dangers of self-consciousness and egotism? Quite simply, love: for God, for our work and for our people. Love has no self-consciousness, no room for pride or timidity, no time for gush. Its own reality protects it from the personal foibles that might corrupt it. When we think of the people we address, their needs and unspoken sorrows, their precious hopes and half-fearful expectations – the thought of self will be lost in concern for others.

Preaching involves a form of creative contradiction. Each word in that simple Pauline affirmation, 'I, yet not I' must be given its full weight. To be pulled both ways is like being stretched on a rack, you could call it a tiny crucifixion. But by what right do we expect a better fate than the one our Master suffered?

IMITATING A TALKATIVE GOD

I've just argued that you really mustn't imitate any other preacher. Well, here is one almighty exception. As a preacher, you have the most awesome of models, God himself. The preacher imitates a talkative God. The most substantial evidence of this is the universe itself. 'And God said ... and there was.' When lawyers talk about 'uttering' a document, they are following a good precedent for God uttered a universe. If God had no interest in making contact with his creation but sat tight-lipped in heaven like Rodin's *Thinker*, then not just preaching but all religion would be irrelevant. For religion is really a summary of all the ways that God and his creation can be in touch.

So the theological doctrines with which you will have to wrestle as you prepare to be a preacher are not stuffy matters to be confined to the lecture room or library as opposed to the heady, exciting stuff of public performance. All preaching is doctrinal preaching because each of the central articles of faith is a way of surmounting some barrier that stands between a talkative God and his creation.

Take the doctrine of the Trinity. It tackles head-on the question: how can a God given to self-disclosure be solitary? Christian orthodoxy insists that the social nature of God is part of his eternal essence; it's not something that developed over time because he began to feel lonely. Our urge to communicate is a God-given human attribute because it is a reflection of the inner dynamics of the Trinity.

Or again, an essential condition for true communication is equality. There can be no act of communication unless we acknowledge our unconditional willingness both to give and to receive. But how is this possible when the encounter is between an omnipotent God and a mortal creature? The answer of Christian doctrine is the Incarnation. As Calvin put it, 'God bends down, and lowering himself, lisps into our ear that we might hear and understand.' The Incarnation is a levelling out of absolute inequalities for the purposes of communication. 'Christ,' says Paul, 'though he was rich became poor so that by his poverty we might become rich,' or as one of the Church Fathers put it, 'he became what we are that we might become what he is. In the communications trade, this would be known as adjusting the frequencies so that voice and ear are on the same wavelength.

But self-disclosure involves all the risks of openness and vulnerability. To come out of the shadows is to present an inviting target, and if it is God who chooses to engage in self-disclosure then he is the most inviting target of all. He who dwells in light unapproachable becomes the one who can be seen, heard and touched. And not all the hands laid on him were loving and respectful. Thus the Cross is the inevitable price of God's self-disclosure. It was perfect communication at infinite cost. The technical term for Christ's saving work is Atonement, personal relationship in total harmony without barrier or distance. And the proof text of Atonement, 'God was in Christ reconciling the world to himself' is an image of parties coming into complete alignment after all distortions have been clarified.

Then again, a system of communication rather than a sporadic burst of messages passing hither and thither requires a network or grid with some degree of permanence. The Christian grid is the Communion of the Holy Spirit. In Bishop John Taylor's phrase, the distance between believers is bridged by the Go-between God, it is the Holy Spirit which powers the system.[13] And the fruits of the Spirit – love, joy, peace and the rest – are precisely those qualities required to permit self-disclosure without fear of exploitation or manipulation.

Finally, when the gap between the parties is not just bridged but transcended then communication solidifies into communion. There is unity not just of meaning but of life. The Bible doesn't tell us much about the detail of the unimaginable condition where the divine-human communication process is complete; when God has disclosed as much about himself as his creatures can bear. It is a state described by terms such as *kabod* in the Old Testament and *doxa* in the New Testament – glory.

I hope, then, that you will find nothing forbidding or abstruse about the theological and biblical studies on which you now embark as an apprentice preacher. Remember, the rawest recruit to preaching in the pulpit has an authority denied to the most eminent scholar in the lecture room. Christian scholarship only exists to enable you as a preacher to do your job. Biblical scholars and theologians are charged with the duty of making it easier for the Gospel to be heard in our time; anything else they do is strictly academic business.

Indeed, all theology is meant to be preached; any doctrine which is so complex or abstruse that it cannot be rendered into sermon form is as near irrelevant as makes no odds. What this means in practice is that at some point in preparing a sermon the preacher must ask, 'What Christian doctrine is this sermon intended to illuminate?' And if the answer is 'None' then the preacher is at sea without a compass.

Yet preachers must be prepared to take responsible risks and proclaim boldly big truths that the professional theologian dare only assert provided he or she is allowed half a page of footnotes. Of course, the preacher mustn't fly in the face of sound scholarship or play fast and loose with it, but there are times when he or she must take a chance and go beyond its more cautious findings.

But also note that the preacher deals with theology in a special way. In the second of his letters to the Corinthians, Paul talks of Christians as 'true deceivers', a paradoxical role which especially applies to preachers. For the faith has to be expressed in ideas that are imprecise and in words that are crude and often misleading. The medium is inadequate for its purpose, but that's the perennial problem of all artists including the preacher.

Take a painter who has to capture life in the round on a two-dimensional canvas. Thus, in the painting, the rows of houses on each side of a street appear to meet at a point on the horizon, whereas we know that in real life parallel lines never meet. The artist must picture things as they *seem* rather than as they *are* in order to state some truth about them. Or a portrait artist may have to decide between capturing a likeness or a character. And often character can only be conveyed by distorting in subtle ways the features of the subject. Possibly the most famous example in recent times was Graham Sutherland's portrait of Winston Churchill which after a decent interval Lady Churchill insisted on destroying because she felt it was a grotesque caricature. On the other hand, discerning critics felt that Sutherland had captured Churchill's dogged aggressiveness and ferocity to perfection. Were they to talk in Pauline terms they would probably call the work a true deception.

Preachers are true deceivers because they are required to simplify incredibly complex issues and speak of them with a confidence that borders on the foolhardy. We are true deceivers when we deal with the Creation in a twenty-minute sermon, disposing of an issue cosmic scientists have wrestled with for generations. We are true deceivers when we proclaim that God became man to redeem the world from evil. The idea of eternity entering time is intellectually absurd, which is why theologians have tied themselves in knots trying to explain how Christ could be both fully human and fully divine. One has only to read the Athanasian Creed with a sceptic's eye to see the problem. Yet in declaring that the Word became flesh, we preachers are true deceivers in order to make an incredible truth believable.

And when we preach that Christ died to save us from our sin we are way beyond our depth. Think of all the theories of the Atonement evolved throughout Christian history, none of which the Church has officially endorsed because even the most profound collapses under the intolerable weight of a reality it cannot contain. Yet we must plough on trying to reduce a great mass of theological doctrines to simple, vivid, compelling truths.

Just as the artist's two-dimensional canvas cannot cope with parallel lines without inspired invention, so the preacher's words and ideas are pathetically unequal to the task of expressing the majesty of divine truth. But we must do our best and get as near to the heart of the matter as we can, relying on God to bridge the gap.

All this at least suggests that there is in preaching a degree of risk and daring which would redeem any life from mediocrity. We cannot always remain in the broad heartlands of faith but must sometimes venture to the dangerous edge of things. But we must be sure of the centre so that if we get hopelessly lost we can find our way back. And it is the intelligent use of the Bible which ensures that we don't completely lose our bearings. The Bible is both the preacher's chart and charter.

THE PREACHER'S CHARTER

More than anything else, your preaching will be governed by your attitude to the Word of God. The Bible *is* the Word of God, the Bible *contains* the Word of God, the preached Bible *becomes* the Word of God, the Bible *mediates* the

Word of God – these statements or any others that describe what you believe about the Bible will decisively affect both the style and content of your sermons.

I'm sure you already know where you stand on this vital issue of the Bible's authority. You may have adopted a position when you became a Christian or fought your way through to one prayerfully and studiously. I don't need to tell you that every theory of biblical inspiration is fraught with its own peculiar challenge and difficulty, so you will have armed yourself with a shelf of good Bible commentaries. You are in for some hard study.

P. T. Forsyth wasn't keen on the phrase that the Bible contains God's word; he felt the truth was much more majestic – God's word contains the Bible.[14] The preacher is driven back to the Bible in order to find out what the Bible goes back to. For it is indubitably true that something was making Christianity and moulding New Testament faith before a single word of the New Testament had been written down. What, then, is behind the Bible and uses it? What is it that is constantly making and remaking the Church? Forsyth insisted that what stands over Bible, Church and creeds is the Gospel of redeeming grace which produced Bible, Church and creeds. The Gospel was an experienced fact, a free, living, preached Word before it was a fixed and written word.

What founded Christianity was not the teaching or even the life of Jesus but the preaching of the theology of his death and Resurrection. It is the foundation of the Kingdom and the essence of the Church's creed, which has only one major clause – God was in Christ reconciling the world to himself – all its other clauses are implicit in that one.

The Bible was not intended to be a preprogrammed

compendium of answers to every conceivable problem the human condition can throw up. The notion therefore that preachers ought to have something to say about everything is a perennial heresy. In fact, though the Bible ranges widely over the history and literature and religion of Jews and Christians, its main aim and purpose is quite specific. It is to point the way to the redemption of human beings from sin and selfishness and the attainment of holiness and fellowship with God.

This is really what the Bible is about – not the history of the Jews or the early Christians but the history of our redemption. Forsyth wrote, 'The preacher's charter is not the Bible but that historic act of redemption of which the Bible is a sacrament.' The Bible's infallibility is not of knowledge nor of historical accuracy but of saving power: it never misleads us about the way of salvation.[15]

Biblical preaching, then, is preaching which stays close to the Bible's key ideas – the holiness of God; his demand for ethical righteousness and judgment on sin; our plight as sinners and need for forgiveness and release; the Christ-Event and pre-eminently the Passion, death and Resurrection of Jesus and its significance both for human history and human destiny. We preachers are required to be students of two periods thousands of years apart. We live in the twentieth century so we inevitably share its world-view but we are also confronted with that of the New Testament. We must be sensitive both to the original meaning of the Bible's text and to its possible meanings in our present culture. Lose touch with the first century and our preaching will be unbiblical, lose touch with the twentieth century and it will become irrelevant.

If we preachers are not speaking to the needs of the contemporary world then we have not really heard what the Bible is saying. On the other hand, however concerned we are to be up to date, our concern is not truly biblical unless it stems from the conviction that the Christ-Event of the first century is the key both to understanding and to changing the twentieth century.

Often, the touchstone of the Bible's relevance is not in its offer of an infallible solution to some problem or other but in the challenge of the inescapable questions it poses which rock us back on our heels. From the first page to the last, the Bible interrogates us. Take a few instances at random: God to Adam, 'Where are you?'; Isaiah to his people, 'Why will this nation perish for disobeying God?'; Jesus to any Christian, 'Why do you call me Lord and don't do what I command you?'; Paul to the people of Lystra, 'Why do you put your trust in gods that cannot save?' Note how frequently Jesus begins a statement with a question.

Such formal questions raised in our minds when we read the Bible are special because they require not academic answers but personal responses. God cross-questions us and challenges us not to an interesting discussion but to costly personal action. Of course, there are imperative statements in the Bible, commandments as well as questions, but even they resolve themselves into demands for our free response as intelligent human beings to the Bible's searching examination of us.

Before they enter the pulpit, preachers will have applied to themselves the sermon they propose to preach. They will have confronted the Word of God, been pierced to the heart by it and led to repentance in the face of divine judgment. But they will also have received with thankfulness the Gospel of forgiveness and found great joy in it. Recall how God placed in Ezekiel's hand a scroll and before the prophet could deliver its message to others he had to eat it;

all that was written there had to become flesh of his flesh and bone of his bone; his very life essence. Then and only then could he preach with authority; then and only then could he declare with absolute conviction, 'Thus saith the Lord ...'

At all costs you must be clear where you stand on this question of the Bible. I am not qualified to help you much but the Church is blessed with excellent biblical scholars writing in a popular vein who can. As my contribution I would offer you a simple couplet from a popular hymn which seems to me to put it all in a nutshell:

Teach me to love thy sacred word,
And view my Saviour there.

PREACHING AS AN ART FORM

Preaching is one of the performing arts and conforms to the rules that govern any art, though there are some important differences which I'll mention in due course. An art is a creative skill by means of which the human imagination and intellect are brought to bear on some medium, words, paint, marble, musical notes, in order to delight or enrich us.

The human mind is not so much a debating chamber where we argue about ideas as a picture gallery around which we hang our images of the world. Human beings can dream dreams and see visions and it is out of this rich but insubstantial stuff that all art in general and our preaching in particular originates. Words in a book are dead, even in the most sacred book. They are paper and print and glue. But when the preacher brings to bear his imagination upon them, they come to life again. Their colour and vigour and glow are the result of the preacher breathing upon hot coals so that once more they crackle and spark and blaze as they have done a million times throughout Christian history.

Art has its own integrity. In the preface to her famous radio play, *The Man Born to Be King*, Dorothy L. Sayers wrote: 'A work of art which is not good and true as art is not good or true in any other respect, and is useless for any purpose whatsoever ... even for edification ... because it is a lie, and the devil is the father of such.'[16] Therefore, one test of a good sermon is that it is also good art.

Yet genuine art never calls attention to itself; it gives no impression of 'artiness'. The artist wants those who see or hear his work to see what he saw, he's not interested in their admiration of his technique. Indeed, if his technique gets in the way and becomes a debating point, some of the impact he strives to make must be lost. This applies equally to preaching as an art. Will the congregation be able to see and feel the truth as you saw it when you were inspired to create your sermon or will its attention be distracted by the nuts and bolts of preaching? Why this illustration? Where did you get that idea from? What a strange turn of phrase that was! If questions such as these are raised in the congregation's mind, the preacher is getting in the way of the message.

To classify preaching as one of the arts is in no way to belittle or vulgarize it. Considered solely in human terms, preaching is high art. It is a vocation doubly vindicated both by a divine call and human achievement. Yet there is one way that preaching does not conform to the rules of art, or rather transcends them for a greater purpose. In its classical definition, all true art is an end in itself, standing on its own as an enriching experience. In general, beauty is its own justification, and there are forms of oratory where elegance of language, purity of voice and grace of gesture excite our admiration even though we find the orator's theme uncongenial or even repugnant. But a sermon can never be an end in itself, merely a means to a greater end. It is a tool and not an ornament, and to judge it by the canons of artistic appreciation alone is to behave like the tribe who were so overawed by electricity that they began to worship the portable generator as God and power cables as his angels. Art for its own sake may be a splendid cultural ideal but it is not one we preachers can share.

The artistic appreciation of sermons was probably at its height in seventeenth- and eighteenth-century France where preachers such as Bousset and Louis de Bourdaloue had such oratorical brilliance that the nobility went to hear them purely as an aesthetic experience, much as they would visit a theatre or watch a great painter at work. The King invited a succession of these pulpit orators to preach before him at Versailles, choosing them not for their spiritual quality but for their wit, eloquence and *esprit*. So pervasive and fashionable did such 'pretty preaching' become that Fenelon in France and Bishop Warburton in England found it necessary to warn against the perils of 'eloquence', sermons that appealed not to the awakened conscience but to the artistic sensibilities of the congregation.[17]

I doubt many people these days are likely to beat the doors of the churches down in order to get in and hear our 'pretty' sermons. For sheer entertainment, the sermon compares decidedly unfavourably with the pop concert or football match. Nonetheless, it is worth taking note of the perils of clever preaching for its own sake. Just as a hymn with a catchy tune can have an unwary congregation bellowing happily about the prospect of its imminent damnation because the beguiling harmonies overwhelm the plain meaning of the words, so harsh truths can be made wrongly palatable by the choice use of words, an elegant sermon structure, gripping illustrations and shafts of wit. Dante wrote, 'I have never used a word solely for rhyme's sake.' He wasn't interested in art for art's sake nor would he sacrifice truth to style.

Oratory is the art of moving people whereas preaching is the art of moving them to a higher life. That is its goal, the purpose by which its effectiveness is to be judged. Sound structure is important for a persuasive sermon, but some of the most powerful sermons have been virtually shapeless; graceful language counts for much, yet some influential advocates of the Christian faith have been innocent of the rules of grammar and syntax, of limited vocabulary and awkward in speech. The aim of a sermon, said Leslie Weatherhead, is to make God real and to change the lives of men and women by the power of Christ. If a sermon does *that*, then any deficiencies measured by the standards of good homiletics mean nothing.

Because a lively imagination is part of the preacher's essential equipment, we touch here on an obvious link between personality and preaching. As a general rule, boring sermons are the product of unimaginative personalities. And such dullness of personality is not an affliction of nature like colour blindness or tone deafness. It is the end result of mental laziness, spiritual lassitude and an unwillingness to take risks with ideas or relationships; in a word, a refusal to feed our imagination on the rich variety of human experience, events and personalities God throws across our path.

There *are* preachers who are so seized by the gravity of their task that they confuse dignity with dullness. Dignity purchased at the expense of suppressing a lively imagination which would bring vitality and brightness and animation to our sermon is a false solemnity. It is the preacher's duty to make his or her sermons so interesting that the congregation far from having to make an effort to concentrate on what is being said would have to make an even bigger effort to concentrate on anything else.

'Boredom', writes Professor Fred Craddock, a preacher who could not be boring if his life depended on it, 'is a form of evil ... It works against the faith by provoking contrary thoughts or lulling to sleep or draping the whole occasion with a pall of indifference and unimportance ... Be honest: have you ever quietly cheered when a child fell off a pew or a bird flew in a window or the lights went out? Passengers on cruise ships, after nine beautiful sunsets and eighty-six invigorating games of shuffleboard, began to ask the crew hopefully, "Do you think we might have a storm?" '[18]

Preaching is not art for art's sake. The lasting impression the preacher should leave in the congregation's mind is not that it has been shown a great demonstration of the preacher's art but that it has been shown a great God.

THE PREACHER AS POET

Let's pursue this line about preaching as an art form a little further. The preacher and poet have much in common because both are concerned with words intended primarily to be heard rather than read; words not chosen simply to describe but to move; words which convey power as well as knowledge. Coleridge described poetry as the best thoughts in the best words: that goes for preaching too.

Now, in yoking together the preacher and the poet I am not (God forbid) suggesting you become an exponent of flowery language or quote poetry copiously in your sermons. Indeed, I think it is a sound rule only to recite poetry in a sermon if it isn't possible to find any other way of saying the same thing, for the purpose of poetry is to express the otherwise inexpressible.

The language of the pulpit like the best poetry ought to have a certain sense of style, not self-consciously preachy or pretentious but elegant, fitted to its high purpose. This comes from practice, practice and more practice. One of my complaints about too much modern theological writing, contemporary liturgy and hymnody is not that they are bad but they *are* bare, short on style. The language is too flimsy to bear the weight of mystery; unable to feed the imagination; as thin as workhouse gruel.

I'm not suggesting you should cultivate a special language in the pulpit you would not employ out of it – if anything, I'm advocating the reverse. It is probably our normal speech that needs some attention so there is no jarring contrast between our spoken style in the pulpit and on the street. An old friend of mine, the late Harry Morton who was General Secretary of the British Council of Churches, taught me that lesson. In and out of the pulpit he used the same pure, elegant English. Hence, when his eloquence reached its awesome height in his sermons there was a continuity of style with his everyday conversation – no one could accuse him of preachiness.

Preaching like poetry seeks to handle the truth with style. George Herbert described his ideal preacher, 'When he preaches he procures attention by *all possible art*.' And the human faculty central to all art is the imagination. By the power of our imagination we can conjure into being what lies beyond, beneath and above the range of our natural eye. It is the imagination which makes connections, uniting things that otherwise would remain unrelated. In this sense it can create a whole world out of isolated bits of our experience.

Can we really get any impression of the mighty sweep of God's Kingdom from a number of texts? We are lost unless our imagination can play upon such biblical evidence as we are given. But we must not do violence to the plain meaning of Scripture in the interests of artistry; the soaring imagination is not a more exciting alternative to the painstaking study of the Bible. Once we have dealt honestly with the text and its context, *then* we can allow it to stimulate our imagination.

Except through the dedicated use of the imagination, how could the preacher talk at all about the God who is by definition beyond human comprehension? It is our imagination which searches out images or turns of speech or illustrations within our experience which point us to a reality utterly beyond it. Metaphor is the technical term for the result in words of using our imagination to light up an elusive truth with the aid of a familiar image. Our descriptions of God abound in metaphor because they are the best we can do. We characterize God as Father, King, Mother, Light, Power, and we follow the New Testament in describing Jesus as Bread, Vine, Shepherd, Door, Way, Alpha and Omega, Resurrection and Life.

Take such metaphors out of the Bible and its colour would seep away and its living spirit vanish. After all, the Bible as the source-book of Christian preaching is of a finite size and even then not all of it is preachable, except by the most perverse use of human ingenuity. Yet it has inspired millions of sermons throughout Christian history. In human terms, the play of a disciplined imagination on the biblical text has created this vast repertoire of sermons.

The fundamentalist may raise his hands in horror at the very suggestion that the preacher's imagination must furnish what is lacking from the biblical record, but the indisputable truth is that in spite of the millions of words written and spoken about Jesus of Nazareth we have a full account only of the last week of his earthly life. The Gospels are, in the strict sense, propaganda rather than biography; they were written by men with some very large axes to grind – which is not to say that these four accounts of Jesus have no basis in fact; far from it. But they are the literary deposit of the preaching of the early Church, and we all know that sermons contain much more than the bare recital of fact.

Indeed, one might ask: how did a Galilean peasant become the cosmic Christ; his earthly life an incident in an eternity-long existence; his death the key to a universal scheme of salvation? None of that can be demonstrated by the methods of strict historical research, for these are realities which exist beyond history. Call the discovery of these doctrines the play of a sanctified imagination on such historical evidence as exists or call it the leading of the Holy Spirit – I wouldn't quarrel with either way of putting it; I suspect they are two forms of the same truth.

One of my complaints about biblical literalism is that it turns the poetry of the Bible into arid prose. The Scriptures issued from a people whose habits of mind and forms of speech were highly poetical and we must take full account of that in interpreting them. Hence, we do less than justice to the profundity of biblical thought, for example, by treating a fragment of a poem charged with Eastern imagination as a sober scientific account of the sun and moon standing still. The inspired visions of Daniel and Ezekiel are not railway timetable-style accounts of a pre-programmed future, nor are the fevered dreams of the Apocalypse coded messages from on high. Not only does this approach ignore serious biblical scholarship, it tramples underfoot the essential poetry of faith, admittedly for worthy motives – but unthinking brutality is no less destructive than the premeditated sort.

Like all Eastern teachers, Jesus spoke a language rich in metaphor and literary imagery; rarely can we get the point by taking his words at face value. I find it curious therefore that fundamentalists insist on the literal interpretation of words which Jesus intended metaphorically in order to stimulate our imagination in the search for the truth which is beyond words. It is as though we were to respond to Robert Burns' claim that his love is like a red, red rose by wondering whether she'd benefit from a spell with a pair of pruning scissors and a helping of horse manure.

Isaac Walton describes John Donne's preaching gift in this way, and it can be no coincidence that Donne was a great poet: 'He pictured a vice so as to make it ugly to those who practised it; and a virtue so as to make it beloved even by those that loved it not.'[19] That's how preaching works; it grips our imagination, then convinces our reason, arrests our conscience and finally reinforces our will, so that stage by stage we have made a fully human response to God's word.

Note the way biblical truth takes wings when it moves beyond the reason into the realms of imagination. Consider the change of emphasis between one verse and another in a single chapter of the epistle to the Hebrews. The author writes, 'Faith is the assurance of things hoped for, a conviction of things not seen.' Yes, well, that's a sound but hardly a soul-stirring affirmation. He then goes on, 'By faith, Abel offered a richer sacrifice ... By faith Abraham obeyed God's call to go forth to a place which he would receive as an inheritance ...' and so on and on. Now we *see* what the writer is getting at; the definition has become a series of pictures. Job put the whole thing in one sentence, 'I had heard of thee by the hearing of the ear; but now mine eye seeth thee ...'

John Ruskin once pointed out that the greatest thing a human being does in the world is to see something and to tell what he or she saw in plain language. He says that hundreds of people can talk for one who can think, and thousands can think for one who can see. 'To see clearly is religion and poetry – all in one,' he claimed.[20] To see, and then to make the congregation see – that is the imaginative gift, one of the central tasks of preaching.

To see what? Well, mostly, truths that have sunk into the congregation's collective unconscious through overfamiliarity, for unlike earlier generations of preachers, we rarely get the opportunity to preach to those totally unfamiliar with the Gospel. Considering the number of sermons to which the average congregation has been exposed it might truly cry with the author of Ecclesiastes, 'There is nothing new under the sun.'

But that's all right. Note how often the phrase 'You all know', or its equivalent, occurs in the apostolic preaching according to the New Testament. It was not an utterly strange message that burst upon the first century. As Dr Johnson said, 'People more frequently need to be reminded than informed.' Your task as a preacher is rarely to offer a congregation a theme of startling novelty; it is much more difficult – to give new life and urgency to what is in danger of becoming hackneyed and stale. And this is where a rich imagination is required. 'Thy laws have become my songs,' said the Psalmist. To make the truths of religion lyrical, that's the ideal.

AMATEURS AND PROFESSIONALS

We've agreed that preaching is one of the performing arts and in all areas of public performance there are amateurs and professionals. This distinction often means not simply that what one does for a living the other does for fun, but often the terms imply different standards of accomplishment. In some areas of the Church, there is a common tendency to regard ordained ministers as professional preachers and their lay colleagues as amateurs who occupy the substitutes' bench and only get a chance to kick the ball when there aren't enough professionals to go round.

Yet Christianity began as a lay religion, and that's how it has been at its best. This is why Protestantism made a battle-cry of 'the Priesthood of all Believers'. And it was a somewhat starchy priest of the Church of England, John Wesley, who unlocked the great power of the laity and organized them into societies where they got on with the job of looking after each other and serving the community with very little help from the clergy. One present-day outworking of this strategy is that the vast majority of nonconformist pulpits this coming Sunday will be occupied by lay preachers.

But there is even more impressive evidence of the importance of lay witness in the pulpit. With the exception of Ezekiel, the great Old Testament prophets were all laymen, and their targets were often the priests who protected the vested interests of temple and shrine. The moral indignation that runs through the history of the Judaeo-Christian religion is as much a layman's indictment of the complacency and outright corruption of the religious professional as of the wickedness of the world.

Amos gloried in his amateur status – 'I was no prophet,

neither was I a prophet's son: but I was a herdsman, and a gatherer of sycamore fruit; and the Lord took me as I tended my flock.' He learned his trade not in the theological seminary but alone in the wilderness, caught up in the hazards of nature. It was this physical setting, his workplace, that fired his mind to shape those prophetic images he used to such powerful effect – justice flowing like a stream, locusts ravaging green shoots, a man running from a bear, the glory of the heavens, the terrifying power of the storm, the majesty of the rocky heights from which he surveyed Edom and Moab – from these Amos derived his sermon material.

The ministerial preacher may benefit from a longer and more systematic training but the lay preacher has an infinitely more varied source from which to quarry the raw stuff of sermons – the secular world – that is where the laity live and move and have their being. For instance, the natural focus of your thinking cannot be liturgics or systematic theology or ecclesiastical history or even the politics and gossip of church assemblies because you have a living to earn as a solicitor – the cry of the community for justice must fill your waking hours.

Obviously, I'm not suggesting that priests and ministers are preserved from all the temptations and challenges of daily living, but over the centuries the Church has evolved structures which to some extent shelter its professional servants. Take the matter of job security, a much greater worry for the laity than the ministry, though some clergy have been made redundant in recent years. It isn't the clergy's fault that the Second Coming didn't come and so an apocalyptic fellowship became an institution and had to succumb to the laws of economics. It is the same Gospel that bridges the infinite distance between the first century Thessalonians giving away all their goods because they expected Christ's return at any moment and the Church Commissioners investing (and sometimes losing) hundreds of millions of pounds in order to keep the clergy in a state of what might charitably be called faded gentility.

But without doubt, the fact that in these straitened economic times many of the laity may be declared redundant at any moment gives an added edge of authenticity to their invitation for a congregation to embrace creative insecurity for the Gospel's sake. The problem with the parson's prophetic pronouncements is that the hand he raises one day in fearless denunciation of the Church must be held out the next day to receive a pay packet.

Another distinction between lay and ministerial preaching derives from the fact that the parson has somehow got to harmonize his or her dual role as prophet and priest. I'm not thinking of the tension *between* prophets and priests in the ministry, that's a squabble with an honourable ancestry which goes back to Moses and Aaron. I mean the tension between the priest and prophet in every minister.

You can see how this tension arises. The minister is servant of an historical Word in the sense that it refers to unrepeatable events concerned with the life and work, complete and sealed, of Jesus. And it is the priest's role to preserve this tradition and recite it within the Church. But this word is also an apostolic word which needs new voices and accents to tell it forth as God's response to the questions the age formulates, and that is a prophetic task.

If ministers confine themselves to their priestly role, the people are not led forward into that thick darkness where God is. If they stick to their prophetic role they may encourage the people to take an irretrievable step into serious error. This inevitable tension between the priest and prophet in every minister has a decisive effect on the style, range and subject of his sermons. The laity are preserved from this necessary ambiguity.

As a lay preacher, you have a unique combination of strengths and weaknesses, distinctive life-experience and an outlook on things moulded by a secular occupation and its demands. So you must not even think of yourself as a substitute or a second-division performer; there is an authenticity and authority about your distinctive accent through which God's word will sound in the ears of the congregation.

But in the end all preachers, clerical or lay, share the same risk that they have committed themselves to a grand, noble illusion. In this fallen and confusing world, we cannot be absolutely sure of virtually *anything*; least of all, those elusive things we call our beliefs, and if we wait for certainty, we will wait for ever. That, surely, is what faith is all about. We can only follow our star until we see one brighter; this is the price we pay for the passion for truth God has implanted in our innermost being. As Elijah told the people of Israel, 'If the Lord be God, follow him, but if Baal, then follow him.' That is the stark choice all Christians face constantly – the possibility, the bare possibility, that a greater Baal may seduce us from our first love. We can only retain the truth of the Gospel by constantly reacquiring it. Faith is a continuous inner warfare.

Some theories can be proved or disproved in five minutes; others might take longer than a lifetime. God, eternity, the purpose of the universe, the meaning of life – these are big questions. By the time I *know* the truth about them beyond a reasonable shadow of a doubt, there may not be much left of my earthly span in which to enjoy my near-certainty. However, it is a great reassurance to us that Jesus himself recommended risk-taking as a jumping-off point for faith. The first demand he made on his followers wasn't that they should worship him or think beautiful thoughts about him but that they should follow him – 'Do what I command,' he insisted. In other words, he's saying, act like a believer and see what happens.

Only on the day of judgment or such other dénouement as the universe determines will it be revealed whether we have been vindicated or exposed as living in a fool's paradise. So be it. At the very least, religion has given point and purpose to our lives, caused us to stand as best we can for the good, the beautiful and the true and add a mite to the amount of love in the world. This is part of religion's perennial appeal – there is hazard as well as comfort in it, the gamble that the darkness of the unknown is filled with God rather than nothingness. Religious believers live by hope, trusting that their risky decision for faith is matched by God's risky decision to disclose something of himself.

In such a problematic enterprise, all lesser distinctions, between parsons and lay preachers, amateurs and professionals, cease to have any real significance compared to the ultimate gamble we and all Christians take. All that we have and are is vested in the truth of the Gospel. If that light should prove to be darkness, then as Paul puts it, we have been fools for Christ's sake. It is this unpredictable element in the religious life which gives preaching its unnerving yet exhilarating sense of flirting with danger. Ministers and laity alike sink or swim together.

THE PERFECT PREACHER?

Earlier I suggested that at least in one sense the preacher imitates a talkative God. One of the college lecturers given the task of teaching me the art of preaching always insisted that Jesus was the ideal model for any preacher. He rhapsodized that Jesus was the perfect communicator, clear, vivid and simple, his artistry supremely demonstrated in the style and structure of the so-called Sermon on the Mount. I have never understood this claim, though to this day I still hear it made. It seems to me that any young preacher who slavishly modelled his or her pulpit style on that of Jesus would be rewarded by congregations dwindling in size and baffled in attitude.

Leaving aside the point that all we know of Jesus' preaching from the Gospels is a literary reconstruction of what the apostles remembered of his oratory, in no conventional sense of the term was Jesus a preacher at all. Utter clarity? Every theological college library has shelves groaning with volumes whose common theme might be paraphrased as 'What did Jesus mean by *that*?' Take just one example: his reference to the sin for which there shall be no forgiveness. What was it? To spend half an hour with the Bible commentators is to stagger away with a thick head. All they seem to be agreed on is that the meaning is opaque and might refer to this, or on the other hand that, or yet again something else.

So what kind of preaching is this? With utter candour, the Gospels report that Jesus' hearers often went away shaking their heads and trying to work out what he was on about. His own family thought him demented, 'He is beside himself!' they moaned and were all set to put him away in an asylum. John the Baptist in prison couldn't decide from what he'd heard whether or not Jesus *was* the Messiah. No matter how often Jesus warned the disciples of his impending death they were still astounded when it happened. That was certainly one message he did not get across. The crowds who heard him gladly when he was doling out food and healing became a dwindling congregation when he offered only strong words.

Any elegance of structure we find in Jesus' Gospel utterances is likely to be the high sheen resulting from the constant repetition rather than original oratorical refinement. His sayings often seem to have the characteristics of extempore, even naïve, speech; uncalculated, throbbing with dramatic immediacy and spoken without regard for the consequences. And I doubt he gave any thought to the possibility that his words might be preserved for future generations. Nor does he make any concessions to the frailties of human understanding; no neat homiletical structure leads irresistibly from the mundane thought-level most of us inhabit to the higher realms of truth.

The American New Testament scholar Amos Wilder wrote this about the public speech of Jesus, 'His utterance is dynamic, actual, immediate, reckless of posterity; not coded for catechists or repeaters. It is live face-to-face communication ... The earliest Christians lived on the free bounty of God. The speech of the Gospel was thus fresh and its forms novel and fluid; it came and went with the freedom of sunshine, wind and rain. Jesus spoke as the birds sing.'[21]

No conventional preacher could speak as the birds sing, we could never display that degree of spontaneity because we are under authority. And one reason why Jesus could speak as the birds sing was because he wasn't a classical orator but a countryman with a rough tongue and a distinctive brogue. He talked like a countryman about the weather and soil cultivation and animal husbandry. Robust images such as those of rotting corpses burying one another or pearls flung before ritually unclean animals or dirty cups being washed on the outside leaving the greasy inside surfaces untouched or of open-flame lamps being hidden under inflammable straw mattresses; a religious man gagging on a fly in his throat after having managed to swallow a camel, its sinuous hairy neck, enormous hump, long bony legs and ungainly hooves – all these images demonstrate the cartoonist's genius for making a point in a rapid vivid sketch.

Jesus drew unforgettable pictures which burn themselves into the mind – hypocrites sounding trumpets in the synagogues, the man with a log in his eye pointing out the speck in his neighbour's, blind men confidently leading their blind companions into the ditch, the nagging widow who gets her way because she pesters the judge to distraction, graphic images used to drive home a serious point about the nature of God and his Kingdom.

His was a vivid imagination fed by acute observation. But this rich imagery wasn't incorporated into what could be regarded as sermons in the normal sense. The scale, style and content of his speech is strictly inimitable. And so it should have been. If he truly was, as the title of one of Bishop John Robinson's books puts it, 'The Human Face of God', we would expect Jesus to look out at the world through very different eyes from natural man or woman; to make judgments according to alien rules and to speak in riddles. For if as God says, 'My thoughts are not your thoughts,' then the way those thoughts are expressed ought at least to sound somewhat strange to our ears.

I've always thought there's profound theology in that old saying that truth is stranger than fiction. Truth is given; fiction we can always invent. Fiction is the product of a human mind which will work overtime to make a story congenial and understandable to other minds. But truth is a different matter. Because its source is outside ourselves, we must either accept it in whatever form it presents itself to us or turn it into fiction to make it more believable.

For the very best of motives, we preachers are prone to turn shocking truth into acceptable fiction. Whenever we come across an enigmatic saying in the Gospels, in order to make sense of it we are tempted to bend it a little, trim it at the edges, paraphrase it judiciously or even claim access to Jesus' mind and insist that he was speaking metaphorically. We rob his words of the trauma of the transcendent. We turn Jesus into the greatest teacher or preacher there ever was and in our naïvety imagine we are paying him some kind of compliment.

A visitor to an art gallery confronted with a painting whose title, *Sunset over Battersea* is the only recognizable thing about it, can do a number of things. He can turn it upside down or sideways to check it has been hung correctly in the first place. He can take a bus at dusk to Battersea, find the exact spot from which the artist painted the picture and try to match his own perception with that of the painter. What he cannot do is change the painting's title to *Scrambled Eggs*, insisting that this is really what the artist was portraying.

The artist may be a genius or a colour-blind dauber in a high fever, but it is his way of looking at something and recording what he sees that is sovereign. By all means advise him to see a doctor or to take up another hobby, but there is no point in trying to convince him that he was really painting something different from what he claims.

Now we preachers tend to behave in a similar fashion when we collide with the more puzzling sayings or inexplicable actions of Jesus in the Gospel. And it is not an option open to us. It is the artist's perception of Battersea, or in this case, Jesus' understanding of the Kingdom of Heaven that is sovereign. And we must either adjust our perspective to see things through his eyes or be done with the whole business, but we cannot trim down his vision to our expectations. We are called to be heralds not propagandists.

Great biblical scholars who are so familiar with the text of the Gospels that they could recite them word for word have confessed that after a lifetime's study, some truths continue to elude them whilst others break in on them unexpectedly. Long-familiar words, pondered a thousand times, inexplicably become charged with fresh meaning when they are studied yet again. It was G. K. Chesterton who wrote, 'You can look at a thing ninety-nine times but if you look at it for a hundredth you are in danger of seeing it for the first time.'[22]

It's hard to resist the conclusion that the basic purpose of Jesus' preaching was not to enlighten us but to shock us awake, to rock us out of the comfortable tramlines of our habitual existence and get us to face another way. So he does absolutely nothing to make his words more palatable or his meaning plain. He doesn't attempt to smooth over the disjunction between things divine and things human or lead people forward from one to the other by gentle steps.

In truth, if we judge Jesus by the usual standards of public oratory, we would sadly have to conclude that he was a failure. As the prologue to John's Gospel puts it, 'He came unto his own and his own received him not.' His gracious invitation, 'Come unto me,' fell on deaf ears until it was enacted from a cross. Not 'Come unto me' but 'I if I be lifted up' was the Messianic secret. It was not his raised voice but his raised Cross that had the power to draw all men unto him. On Calvary he preached the final, complete and unequivocal sermon, in almost complete silence.

Unlike his more enigmatic sayings, this word could not be misunderstood. It could be ignored, rejected, but not misunderstood. It was perfect communication at infinite cost.

Hence, the preacher who looks to Jesus as a model had better count the cost. I suppose the point I'm trying to make is that the distinguishing feature of the Christian preacher who seeks to imitate the Nazarene rabbi is not silver-tongued eloquence or elegant sermon structure but the marks he or she bears in their body of the dying of the Lord Jesus.

TWO

THE SERMON

HARD GRAFT

As a preacher, you have embarked on a gruelling task which doesn't get any easier the more experienced you become. I am sure this is the single biggest cause of failure in the modern pulpit – we just don't work hard enough at it. Though it is an art, preaching is also a craft and you master a craft only by hard labour, constant practice, trial and error and the expenditure of much brain power.

It is fashionable these days to deride the approach to preaching advocated by the late Dr W. E. Sangster as too mechanical with its painstaking analysis of sermon types and attention to the elements of what he insisted is a craft. Without doubt, he was right. Just as a badly crafted chair may let someone down, so a botched sermon may let them down with an even bigger bump. Of course all the craftsmanship in the world cannot produce a preacher, but lack of attention to the hard-won skills of the trade may render ineffective even one with natural talent. The more proficient and experienced we preachers become, the more easily we are tempted to take a chance and rely on verbal fluency to get us through.

Preaching is an intellectually demanding task, by which I do *not* mean the preacher must be loaded down with

academic attainments or produce sermons bursting with
abstruse references. Some of the greatest preachers in
Christian history had little formal education but what they
lacked in academic attainments they made up for in holy
wisdom. They reflected deeply on their sermon themes and
put in long, long hours refining them.

The Puritan preacher Richard Baxter confessed he
always preached one sermon over the heads of his people
each year with the aim of keeping them humble and
proving that he could do it every Sunday if he chose. I
like that touch of vanity and innocent cunning in a great
Christian, but for two reasons, our own sermons are
unlikely to fly over our people's heads: first, because by
the law of averages at least half the congregation will be
brighter than we are; and secondly, every honest hour we
spend in preparing a sermon ought to add to its profundity
whilst subtracting from its difficulty. This is what much of
the sweat and blood is for, to produce simplicity and clarity.

Principal Alexander Fairbairn, a turn-of-the-century
scholar, was a preacher of massive intellect whose gift of
language was phenomenal. His sermons were on the grandest
scale and moved in a majestic sweep that left his hearers
breathless. An old Scottish farmer used to drive miles every
Sunday to hear Fairbairn preach and was often chaffed by his
friends for being too dim to understand what he had heard.
He replied, 'Maybe aye or maybe no, but man, it's grand to sit
in the front pew and catch the force of it going past your
lugs.'[23] To 'catch the force of it going past your lugs' is not a
substitute for clear understanding of what is being said but at
least it testifies to the grandeur of the Word of God. Fairbairn
was not prepared to patronize ordinary people; they got the
very best of what was in his mind and spirit.

Paul wrote, 'I pray that your love may abound yet more

and more in knowledge and in all judgment.' Knowledge and judgment; there is no substitute for them, certainly not fervour, fluency or enthusiasm. Knowledge – in that preachers should know as much as they can – and judgment, in deciding to what extent that knowledge should be on display. However much or little of the intellectual scaffolding of a sermon we reveal, the congregation has the right to expect the preacher to have thought through his or her theme so that there are no hidden flaws in the argument, no decisive counterstrokes which could demolish the whole thing.

One of the notes that rings throughout Paul's writings is the immense intellectual satisfaction he derived from the Gospel. Paul was certainly not unemotional but the emotion came after clear intellectual conviction, indeed, sprang out of it. He never spared the minds of those he addressed. He expected them to think, to love the Lord with all their minds as well as with their hearts and strength.

One of his letters would arrive, say, in Rome, and it would be read out in church. Who would his hearers be? Many of them were slaves, probably unable to read or write. Yet he confronts them with rigorous logic and powerful theological ideas. He makes no concessions to popularity; he offers not just spiritual regeneration but an intellectual awakening, a great mental adventure.

It is fatally easy for us preachers to be slipshod and offer only half-digested arguments, illustrations aimed at emotional effect rather than specific illumination, material we have borrowed without acknowledgment, oratorical intensity which owes more to our glands than our deepest convictions, apparent spontaneity of gesture and expression craftily premeditated. We are taking the easy way out; we know it and sooner or later the congregation will sense it also.

What I am suggesting is that much present-day preaching

lacks intellectual energy. I don't believe the intellectual case for Christianity is the only or even most important one, but there is a comprehensiveness, profundity and even beauty about the way Christian doctrines interlock and spell out the Gospel, and we really have to work at the task of doing them justice.

The preacher must, however, be aware of the limits to Christian explanation. Christianity does not make the mistake of trying to explain away everything. It observes a proper reticence about the strictly mysterious element in life – not what is as yet unknown until the Big Brains get around to unravelling it, but what will remain for ever unknowable. There is mystery to be found not beyond the present frontiers of knowledge but existing at the heart of the simplest things and everyday experiences.

Like Jacob at the ford at the River Jabbok we wrestle with one who is beyond the range of our senses, who comes to meet us from dazzling darkness, only if and when he chooses. God's self-disclosure is always veiled; it is never without ambiguity. When his opponent leaves him, Jacob is still not *quite* sure with whom he has been dealing. 'Why do you want to know my name?' the stranger asks. Jacob believes he has met God and lived to tell the tale, but he doesn't *know* that beyond a shadow of a doubt. The mystery has not been dispelled.

'Mystery' – the Greek term means to close one's mouth – for every attempt to capture its essence in words is doomed to failure. Therefore, leave plenty of room in your argument for what Paul called knowledge in a mystery. And one way to preserve the mysterious element in preaching is to avoid the temptation to be too tidy-minded. We must acknowledge honest doubt and avoid pat answers to agonizing issues which can be perfectly resolved only in the mind of God. I am not suggesting you should cultivate deliberate vagueness or obscurity of thought, but do not make great things small, holy things common or costly things cheap. Don't try to wrap up great sprawling realities in neat verbal parcels or seek in twenty minutes or so to resolve, once and for all, enigmas that have baffled the greatest minds.

In the transaction between God and the congregation of which the preacher is one channel, what is being passed on is not explanation of any kind but life, and not just life but divine life in Christ who is the communicated self-expression of God. So as you begin to prepare your sermons, be assured that nothing less than this is at stake.

STICKING TO THE FACTS

I've insisted that preaching is an art form, nevertheless it's firmly anchored in the real world, so as you begin to think about constructing a sermon, always bear in mind that Christianity rests upon a finite number of facts. There are great religions where the truth of what is taught is not affected by whether its gods and heroes ever lived within history. By contrast, Christianity does stand or fall on the fact that Jesus of Nazareth was, as the Apostle's Creed states 'crucified under Pontius Pilate' – that is, somewhere in the narrow stretch of history between AD 26 and 36 during which Pontius Pilate was governor of Judaea.

The Gospel you are called upon to preach is based upon a number of facts, and it is important that you do not emphasize any of them at the expense of the others. Many of the Church's tragic divisions have been caused by zealous Christians who, believing that a doctrine was suffering neglect, proceeded to exalt it, generally to the exclusion of others. The constant harping of some evangelicals upon the Cross; the narrow insistence of some theological liberals upon the Kingdom of God; the massive emphasis of some Pentecostals on the Holy Spirit. The motives are worthy but such doctrinal obsessiveness can tear asunder the wholeness of the Gospel.

The true preaching of the Gospel requires that the totality of the Jesus-Event should be spelt out; all facts must be given their due emphasis. I shall have more to say later about the danger of the preacher becoming a one-string fiddler, but for the present I urge you to recognize thankfully and to observe assiduously the Church's liturgical year. This will ensure that you give attention to each of the central doctrines of the faith – though let the calendar be, as the hymn puts it, your guide and not your chain. You must not allow it to become a straitjacket or a set of pigeonholes into which great doctrines are popped and left to wait until they are taken out, dusted off and preached again at the appropriate season of the following year.

So, whilst I welcome the discipline imposed by the liturgical year, I must not allow it to render me unadventurous. I cannot recall preaching a Christmas sermon in high summer, and I suspect that if I did a congregation would think I was suffering from mental confusion. What about Pentecost in autumn, Ascension in the bleak midwinter? Why not? These doctrines are universally relevant; the truths they attest do not fluctuate in importance according to the calendar. We should also recognize the efficacy of all the great Christian doctrines. For instance, the doctrine of the Cross has no monopoly of converting power, surely the Resurrection also has life-changing significance? And the Christian activist might give some attention to what is often loosely called the Second Coming of our Lord, for divested of some its more garish imagery it has profound political and social consequences.

The facts on which the Christian faith is based may be finite in number but the permutations and combinations expressed in terms of doctrines provide an almost endless variety of preaching themes. Let the preacher take an axe to the pigeonholes and allow the Spirit to have its sway. The only warning I would sound is that the limits of preaching are set by the Bible and not by the exercise of sanctified imagination on the part of a preacher who is determined to be different at any price.

Let me take the argument a stage further: the facts upon which the Gospel is based are facts of a special kind – they are *decisive* facts because they demand some response from the hearer. There are certain facts I can take or leave as I choose. I find it hard to get het up about the fact that the planet Uranus has a mean distance from the sun of 1,783 million miles, nor do Lambert's conformal conic projections set my heart pounding with excitement. But there are facts that may in themselves be neutral in character but become decisive should circumstances change. The comment, 'I see the River Thames flows at the bottom of your garden,' might evoke a polite response from me, whereas the warning, 'That river at the bottom of your garden has overflowed its banks!' will set me off at a gallop.

Thus, the whole point of preaching is that when we have defined, dissected and analysed Christianity in every possible way, its key function is to *change* something or rather, someone. At the heart of every sermon must be thrusting challenge, the articulation of God's imperious demand, the offer of his forgiveness and the gift of his grace.

Textbooks of homiletics often talk about 'preaching for a verdict'. I don't think the phrase is a happy one because it has about it the smack of the argumentative, the litigious, though the basic idea is sound. As a solicitor, you know well that it's possible to win a verdict in a law court by sheer brilliance, outright lying, twisting the law or appealing to base motives. A verdict need not be derived from the facts, and anyway the argument is addressed to a third party, judge, jury or tribunal. But accepting all these qualifications, at least the phrase does serve to remind you that you are not in the pulpit to entertain your hearers or divert them with an interesting discourse. The barrister is about a grave business – if a case is half-prepared or the presentation of the facts is lackadaisical, the whole course of a client's life could be adversely changed for ever.

What follows from the factual nature of the faith? Simply that the core of true preaching is personal experience, for what we call a fact is simply an experienced truth. Experience is the way reality dawns upon us; it is the witness to our contact with the world. The Word of God can only be fully intelligible to those who have felt its full impact upon them. That's what's behind that saying of Jesus, 'Except a man be born again, he cannot see the Kingdom of God.' Only as you live within it can you truly discern its boundaries and dimensions and qualities. No judgment upon it you make from outside as an observer or a spectator is worth very much.

Preaching, then, makes its appeal to what is there, to the facts of faith. It testifies to two levels of experience – *your* experience of God's dealings with you in Christ, and the cumulative experience of the people of God who, with united voice, proclaim that they have found the facts of faith to be reliable. Preaching is based on the given facts of faith, it is neither concerned to add to them nor to indulge in fanciful speculations that go beyond your own experience or that of the Church of God. Personal experience will always be the linchpin of your preaching as you echo the words of the blind man whom Jesus healed, 'This one thing I know, once I was blind and now I see.'

There are some preachers who imagine that once their sermon has been consigned to paper and written out in full they are ready to preach. But all they've got is a manuscript and not a sermon. Not until they have reabsorbed it into themselves and made it their own so that they can say over every dot and comma, 'Yes, I can swear to that!' has a sermon come into being. A religious belief must be true for us before it can become a conviction that is able to be preached.

In this instance, you are the one whom God has called to preach, so presumably it is your experience of him that he wishes you to share with others. And this is the difference between preaching and any other form of exposition that relies on the use of the spoken word such as the oration, the lecture or the recitation. For one period of my life I used to give lectures on Marxism which I hope were fair to a thinker who undoubtedly changed the face of the twentieth century. But my aim was to add to my students' knowledge, it was not to get them to commit themselves to the Proletarian Revolution. But when I preach, my whole aim is to get those who hear me to share my faith.

DOCTRINAL MODESTY

As you ponder a possible sermon theme, let me warn you about a strange thing that seems to have happened to the psychology of the modern Church. Modesty seems to have moved from the organ of ambition and settled on the organ of conviction. We were always intended to be *personally* but not *doctrinally* modest, to underplay our moral virtues but not our spiritual convictions. In our desire to match the scepticism of our age, we have almost become too doctrinally modest to believe in the multiplication table. 'People will never swallow that!' we exclaim as we abandon yet another of the traditional doctrines of the faith, until what is left for people to swallow is not nutritious enough to keep a gnat alive.

There is an understandable fear amongst some Christians that being too assertive about what we believe can easily degenerate into cocky certitude, bigotry, in fact. But this is to misunderstand the nature of bigotry. Bigotry is the anger of those who have no true opinions; it is the frenzy of the doctrinally indifferent. Bigotry is an unholy alliance of passion and ignorance, not a wholesome marriage of passion and truth. Belief is an emotion which has been triggered by an idea; bigotry is an emotion which has been triggered by a hatred of ideas. No one with a care for words is in danger of confusing conviction with bigotry.

It's sad that this outburst of false modesty, this frenzy of doctrinal indifference, is occurring just as a great vacuum has opened up at the heart of a society whose dominant mood has in a few decades swung from self-confidence to impotence. The civilization that split the atom and landed on the moon confesses itself utterly baffled by problems that seem to admit of no solutions; where every alternative is a dead end. No one seems to know what to do about rising crime rates, the irresistible decline of the traditional family, mass starvation, world economic recession, tribal, racial and religious conflicts, irreversible environmental damage.

This is no time for preachers to lose their nerve doctrinally, to offer revised, abridged and simplified versions of the faith. For Christianity has always claimed to address the Big Questions and it is now only the Big Questions that matter, even though our society seems unable to cope with anything other than little answers.

Of course there is much more to Christianity than a scheme of comprehensive explanation, but at the very least it is precisely that, and tackles head-on the two issues which preoccupy most thoughtful people as they survey the moral and spiritual dereliction of our time: 'Why is the world the way it is?' and 'Why am I the way I am?' And what can be done about either?

One is a question about history, the other about human nature. And one of the reasons I am a Christian is that I find the Christian explanation of the glory and tragedy of human nature more compelling than that of the humanist, and its explanation of human history as a tragic interplay of good and evil more profound than that of the Marxist. The Christian case has got to be argued patiently and persistently, issue by issue. Even in the Decade of Evangelism, spiritual fervour is no substitute for sheer brain power. It will not do to hurl biblical texts like missiles at the problems of our society nor apply Jesus as a sticking plaster to its festering wounds. There are no short cuts in Christian apologetics.

Take a few examples of the unfashionable doctrines we tend to play down. The doctrine of original sin seems remote from everyday experience yet where is there a more convincing explanation of the moral enormities that face us in every news bulletin? The doctrine claims that whereas every constituent part of the rest of creation is striving to realize its own nature – thus, every atom of a cabbage is striving to make a decent cabbage – not every constituent part of a human being is trying to make a decent human being. There is a deep corruption of the human will at work in all our affairs which exacerbates those problems it does not actually cause. And this structural defect will not respond to any human artifice but only to a gospel of redemption which has its origins in the being of God himself.

Or there is the question of God's providence. The moment we try to justify God's loving care for his world we find ourselves wrestling with that old-fashioned but critically important term – theodicy – the defence of God's goodness in the face of suffering and evil. For much of the time, the origins of evil and suffering are an intellectual problem only for believers who have to reconcile awful eventualities with any notion of a loving purpose directing things. But sometimes even non-believers find that the sheer scale, impact and destructiveness of the world in uproar forces them to ask the illogical but clamant question: 'How could a God we don't believe in allow such things?'

Theodicy has burst out of the pulpit and theological school largely because the advent of live television will not allow the general public to evade the hard questions raised as a ravaged, violent world implodes into our living rooms. Instantaneously, as they happen, we see the bombs explode, the seas smash the barriers, the buildings crash, the starving children die before our eyes.

It is in the teeth of such appalling realities that we have to argue doggedly for the conviction that the world in its tragedy and grandeur is unfolding as one great divine creative act which only in view of its final purpose makes any sense. And further, the only possible theodicy is to be found in the Cross – which puts catastrophe in its true perspective. The God who spared not his own son will not scruple to bend the most dreadful eventualities to his purposes; he makes the forces that rage against him work to accomplish his ends.

Calvary was both the climax of God's providential care for his world and the supreme crisis of history, more dreadful than any imaginable human catastrophe – earthquake, famine or sword. For it cost God more to redeem the world than to make it in the first place, for our new life was not created out of nothingness but out of wreck. The future can add nothing in principle to the great settlement of good and evil made on Calvary. There is nothing ahead of humanity that has not already been discounted in that encounter on the Cross. This may be a tough doctrine to argue in our time but the alternative is nihilism of the bleakest sort.

Again, all preaching begins from the same datum point, the holiness or 'godness' of God. Thus, when we talk about God's holiness, we are not describing a specific quality like his love or justice. We are talking about that which makes him God. It is possible to conceive a God who is not love or is not just; it is not possible to conceive of a God who is not holy.

In the opening pages of the Bible, God's holiness seemed to have no ethical content. It was raw, sometimes savage energy, and to get in its way was fatal – as that poor chap Uzzah who tried to steady the ark found out, or those two priestly sons of Aaron who were fried to a crisp for indulging in a little unauthorized liturgical revision. In the early dawn of the human exploration into God, his holy otherness at first evoked sheer dread and little else.

Then the prophets made one of the great discoveries in the history of religion, for they detected another element in the holiness of God besides transcendent otherness, and that was moral perfection. Holiness not just as energy but as moral energy; a force that makes for righteousness; a crusading power that seeks to pour out salvation upon the nations. This was a great leap forward but it encompassed a problem. 'God is holy,' said the ancients; 'God is holy *and*

52

yet a saviour,' said the prophets. But that conditional *and yet* involved a paradox. A saviour God calls us to him, a holy God has no option but to repulse us when we get there because of our sinfulness.

Those two elements in the prophetic understanding of the holiness of God were held in creative tension until Jesus resolved the paradox by adding a final link to the chain of argument. 'God is holy,' said the ancients; 'God is holy and yet a saviour,' said the prophets; 'God is holy and therefore a saviour,' said Jesus. Holiness not as raw energy nor as moral energy but as redemptive energy. The paradox of God as holy and a saviour was settled on Calvary where *and yet* gave place to *therefore*. On Calvary, God vindicated the name Jesus had given him – Holy Father. What Jesus had bidden his disciples to pray for – the hallowing of God's name – he demonstrated by his obedience unto death.

It is this element I find missing from much contemporary preaching – not the fatherhood of God, we hear plenty about that, but his holy fatherhood. The difference between loving fatherhood and holy fatherhood is the difference between forgiveness and redemption. A father who is patient and infinitely wise can freely forgive at the cost of grief and wounded affection. It is an individual matter. But a single human being cannot be saved in isolation from a whole world; to redeem us, our sin must be destroyed and that meant not a minor action on God's part but the reorganizing of the universe. We have not just erred and strayed like lost sheep; we have embraced mutiny; the crew have taken over the ship. What is at stake is a diseased world; a society sick unto death. The challenge is not simply to restore the prodigal but to transform the moral condition of the entire household.

There is about the doctrine of God's holy fatherhood a

note of rigour which is far removed from the notion of a benevolent fatherly God, and once our preaching loses the note of the holy it has lost everything.

Finally, a theme which except at Easter has virtually disappeared from Christian argument, that of personal immortality. It was Matthew Arnold who said that no religion can long survive the decay of hope of immortality. Of course, for Christians, the Resurrection of Jesus dominates this issue, yet our general grounds for belief in eternal life are an essential part of the Christian apologetic and should be argued more often than they are. These arguments can be little other than pointers to an ineffable reality, for who has personal experience of the ultimate mystery? We can offer only probabilities, but the great mathematician Clerk Maxwell once said that life is governed by the calculus of probabilities. And no argument is wasted which renders the natural mind hospitable to the truth of the Resurrection.

The higher our estimate of the human spirit, the less credible does it seem that it is intended to burn with a fierce bright flame for only a handful of years before flickering and vanishing. There is nothing rational about a universe which clings to the lowest, inanimate matter and lets the highest, the human personality, go. If the mountain outlasts the one who conquered it; if Bach's manuscripts are more enduring than the mind which conceived them; if the saint's mummified body is preserved but the soul aflame with God which occupied it is no more, then the universe is a moral outrage and an affront to common sense. If that kind of a world would not satisfy us, why should we assume it will satisfy the God from whom our ideas of truth, rationality and justice emanate?

Eternal life in the Christian understanding has never been anchored in any faculty or quality of the human personality but in the nature of God as love. And this must infer immortality of some sort, for love is the drive to unite all that is separated in time, space and condition. And it is obvious that in our brief time-span there are many forms of separation we cannot overcome. We shall meet our death as unfinished creatures, but because we have come to know the love of God, the infinite has been joined to the finite, the work of making us whole has begun and must persist until the enterprise is perfected.

To put it in such spatial language is strictly nonsense, but it makes sense to express the reality of conversion in this way – those who have known the love of God last as long as his love lasts. For whatever we make of Jesus, it's fair to say he died to show us that whoever we are, we matter to God. And since by definition, God must be perfectly consistent, there can never be a time when we cease to matter to him. Therefore we must be the objects of his love eternally. If God loves us, he must love us till the end, not our end but his end, and since God has no end, in the sense of ceasing to be, he must love us eternally.

Of course, such arguments fall a long way short of a fully developed Christian understanding of eternal life. For that, we must add to the equation a factor of a quite different kind, the Resurrection of Jesus not just as a sequel to the gospels, but as the truth in whose light the gospels came to be written at all. The whole point of the Gospel message is that the purposes of God have been accomplished in the life, death and Resurrection of Jesus. And since Jesus has conquered death, all those alive with his life have their deaths behind them in all but the biological sense.

Now for the preacher to be diffident about such doctrines in a time of despair and confusion is much more serious than false modesty; it is dereliction of duty.

FOR GOD'S SAKE, SMILE!

We've been discussing neglected themes in modern preaching, and there is one to which I want to draw your special attention; well, it's not so much a theme as a neglected perspective – the humorous dimension of religion. Let me hasten to add that I'm not thinking of the propensity to tell jokes in the pulpit. There are rare preachers who have that knack, but as a general rule attempts at sermonic jokiness produce only teeth-grinding embarrassment. It was Dean Jonathan Swift who warned, 'Beware of attempting wit in your sermons, for it is very near a million to one that you have none.'[24]

I'm thinking of something rather more subtle. The preacher without a sense of humour is not only seriously handicapped for the business of living but will also be incapable of understanding much of what religion is about. William Hazlitt in a famous essay on humour, writes, 'Man is the only animal that weeps and laughs; for he is the only animal who is struck with the difference between what things are and what they ought to be.' And isn't much preaching taken up with that difference?

There are those who will insist that religion is much too serious a subject to lend itself to humour. Actually, I don't believe that *any* subject is too serious to be funny about, though there are occasions when humour would be an inappropriate or cruel way of dealing with it. If we are probing the outer boundaries of humour, the Nazi concentration camps must surely be the limiting case. Who dare make a joke about them? Is it possible to react to the Holocaust with other than blank horror and despair? Surely it is sacrilegious even to look for evidences of humour in these boiling cauldrons of evil? Well, the truth is that those amazing people, the Jews, have added to their huge treasury of religious wit a whole vein of heroic comedy that came out of the death camps where laughter was the only way by which the inmates could assert their essential humanity.

Some of us do not find it easy to give ourselves permission to laugh about religious matters. We have this deeply-ingrained sense that we should always be serious about serious things and unutterably solemn about the most serious thing of all, God. Yet the words 'funny' and 'serious' are not opposites. The opposite of 'funny' is 'unfunny'; the opposite of 'serious' is 'frivolous'. So religion can be both a serious subject and sometimes a very funny one as well.

But here the preacher comes into collision with a central Christian tradition which has always depicted Jesus as the Man of Sorrows. It's not easy to call to mind any representations of him in classical art which show him roaring with laughter. I know of one exception. In the Victoria and Albert Museum there is or used to be an Italian Renaissance statue of a smiling Madonna with a Child gurgling merrily on her lap. It is called *The Virgin and the Laughing Child* and is so untypical as to attract special attention.

However, we should never forget that Jesus was a Jew. The Word didn't just become flesh in general but took up residence in a particular man, of a given race, at a specific time. And it happened to be a race celebrated throughout its long and eventful history for a gloriously rich legacy of humour. There runs through that Jewish book, the Old Testament, a whole vein of mocking humour attributed to God. In one of the greatest of all religious poems, the book of Job, God bombards Job with a torrent of barbed witticisms. And the crunch of the argument God offers for his existence is not the moral perfection and consistency of his creative order but the sheer pointlessness of parts of it – 'Hast thou not sent the rain upon the desert where no man is?' – the implication being that because God is God he is free to behave not just with complete rationality but also to indulge the playful side of his sovereignty.

Again, there is the account of the discussion between God and Abraham about the birth of Isaac, whose very name means 'Laughter' – the point of the word-play being that God has played a joke on Sarah who to her astonishment becomes pregnant at an advanced age. Then there are Elijah's knockabout tirades against the priests of Baal on Carmel. Or what about that whole chapter of Isaiah given over to a satirical ode about the King of Babylon in which he is the butt of God's derisive glee? Even in the very book of the Bible which warns us against taking the Lord's name in vain, God is described as giggling and winking. And the book of Psalms records God sitting in heaven roaring with laughter.

Note what an important role joyous celebration had in the life of the people of Israel. Nehemiah and Ezra rebuked the Jewish people for being miserable instead of celebrating when they were told what God demanded – 'All the people wept when they heard the words of the law. Then he said to them, "Go your way, eat the fat and drink sweet wine and send portions to him for whom nothing is prepared, for the joy of the Lord is your strength." ' Holiness was all the better for being shot through with joy.

God's transforming power is often described in the Old Testament as turning mourning into joy. The Psalmist advises the people that the appropriate way to praise God is 'with dancing'. The processional dance to the accompaniment of musicians was the usual way of advancing up the sacred mountain, Zion. And the prophets assured the Jews that when they regained their lost sense of divine election they 'would go forth in the dance of the merrymakers'. Indeed, King David was rebuked by his wife for behaving in a vulgar fashion by larking about in front of the Ark improperly dressed. But to those who knew the joy of their salvation, matters of propriety and dignity took second place to spontaneous celebration.

And Christianity has kept alive this humorous vein in religion. For example, cathedrals were built in the great ages of faith, yet they are filled with gargoyles – grotesquely funny stone figures staring down from walls and roof so that when worshippers lifted their eyes towards heaven, they might be struck both by the sense of God's majesty *and* the absurdity of the human condition. Or in some of the medieval morality plays, the spectators engage in silly clowning at the foot of the Cross, and in the York cycle the Roman soldiers preparing the Cross for the Crucifixion bore holes in the wrong places – as a result, Jesus' hands cannot be nailed to its cross-beam.

Religious festivals such as the medieval Feast of Fools were occasions when believers felt able to make fun of all the things, people and rites they took with the utmost seriousness throughout the rest of the year. The monks appointed one of their number Lord of Misrule to preside over a mock Eucharist. He chanted a Litany of Folly during which an ass was worshipped and the communicants brayed their responses. It seems that when people were secure in their religion they could afford to be jokey about it. On the other hand, in a secular age swept by doubt many believers feel threatened when someone pokes fun at their religion.

One possible meaning of the word 'religion' is 'that which binds everything together' – the totality of life united in whatever or whoever we call our God – life and death, time and eternity, spirit and matter, the things which call out tears and those which evoke laughter. You can no more leave out humour from a religious account of the world than exclude the continent of Asia from an inventory of its land masses. We need a humorous perspective on religion to preserve us from making fools of ourselves by according our self-made idols undue respect.

As a preacher you are addressing a society whose distinctive marks are industrial plenty and scientific genius, but it is a society growing stale because it no longer holds any surprises for us. We have subdued the environment to such a degree that our sense of wonder has become redundant like our appendix or that rudimentary tail at the base of our spine. When our heads are bent low over our desks and our energies are harnessed to the business of earning a daily living and doing our social duty we tend to exclude from our consciousness the elements of the uncanny, the absurd and the terrifying. We no longer lift up our eyes towards the hills nor hear the music of the spheres. Indeed, we have to employ our technological virtuosity to indulge ourselves in second-hand thrills by means of X-rated movies or horror videos.

It is when we are in playful, laughing mood that we are particularly sensitive to the wonders of life and grateful for them. We are capable of being astonished at a world full of marvels which happens to be co-extensive with this earthly one. The real wonder as the philosopher Wittgenstein said is not *how* things are but *that* they are. That huge jolly mystic G. K. Chesterton confessed he never ceased to be amazed at the wetness of water, the fierceness of fire, the steeliness of steel and muddiness of mud.[25] The knack of living creatively is both to be at home in the world and constantly astonished at it.

Wonder is evoked by sudden new shafts of light on old realities. And once our eyes are opened we realize we are surrounded by miracles; nature, even at its most down-to-earth, is not natural but supernatural, delighting us with a million marvels. The soul has its sleeping and unvisited parts, a treasure trove of faculties and powers unrecorded in the textbooks, unremarked by historians and too often missed by the theologians. We need only change the wavelength of our perception and we enter a different world. That's what a sense of humour can do – move the needle on the dial of our sensitivity and tune in to a whole dimension of existence that for too long has been excluded from our world-view.

True religion has the power to make us joyful about the most serious things. It is significant that the great epic poem in which Dante offers a comprehensive account of life in the form of an allegory of the human soul's progress towards God is called *The Divine Comedy*. The Psalmist declares that God can cause human wrath to praise him, so it's permissible to assume the Almighty can also sanctify our sense of humour. After all, what about those words of the old Catechism many of us learned by heart as children? – 'What is the chief end of man?' 'The chief end of man is to glorify God and *enjoy* him for ever.' That presumably means that we have been preprogrammed to do just that, enjoy God. It has taken billions of years of evolutionary pain to produce creatures like us who have the power to laugh. We mustn't let the faculty go to waste.

Leo Tolstoy wrote that he became a Christian because he was amazed at the capacity of Christians to be joyous in the face of life and death. For all its emphasis on the Passion and death of Jesus, the New Testament is a happy book and that should be a dominant note in your preaching.

There are some preachers so grave and burdened down with the sin of the world that the first sight of them in the pulpit causes the congregation's heart to sink to its boots. Provided the circumstances are appropriate, enter that pulpit with a lightsome heart, a laughing eye and a benevolent smile, determined to cheer the people by reminding them of the hopeful, positive, joyous aspects of faith and celebrate the Jesus through all of whose teaching runs a gaiety which mocks the prudential and the calculated, who promises us the freedom of a Kingdom where neither misery nor mortality has the last word.

THE CURSE OF ST AMBROSE

I doubt there ever was an excellent preacher who was not in love with words. I'm not thinking about formal education but a feeling for language, a sense of the weight of the word. And it is the *spoken* word the preacher must master. For as Dr Johnson said in the preface of his famous *Dictionary*, 'the pen must at length comply with the tongue'. In the end, the spoken word will prevail. Charles Smyth wrote, 'Anyone can preach effectively who reads his Bible, says his prayers and loves his people.'[26] I would add another clause, 'and cares for words' – the sound, meaning and rhythm of language.

In his *Confessions*, St Augustine says he found St Ambrose doing something without precedent at that time, he was reading without moving his lips and so made no sound. 'When Ambrose read, his eyes moved over the pages, and his soul penetrated the meaning without his uttering a word or moving his tongue. Many times we saw him reading silently and never otherwise ...'[27] Augustine decided this must be either because St Ambrose feared someone might overhear and delay him by demanding an explanation of the text or because he was trying to avoid straining his vocal cords. But the sight of his spiritual master reading in silence troubled Augustine for years afterwards.

Now Ambrose was a great saint and preacher but he did the rest of us preachers no favours when he established the fashion of silent reading, scanning with the eye. For to state the crashingly obvious, the sermon is a speech-event. It may start life in a manuscript or as written notes and eventually find its way into a book or the parish magazine but that is a secondary matter. A sermon in any other form than speech is like unplayed music. A written sermon is merely the corpse of dead proclamation, a lifeless husk. There is about the sermon in essence an immediacy, an urgency, a now-or-neverness no more to be captured in cold print than a sea wave can be trapped in a bottle without being reduced to a pint of salt water.

To draw attention to the now-or-neverness of a sermon is not to ignore the fact that you may well use a sermon on more than one occasion, most preachers do, and in a curious way that proves my point, for it is no longer the same sermon even though you repeat it word for word. A fresh occasion gives it renewed life. It is a new creation because, however subtly, both the preacher and congregation have changed since the sermon was last preached. And the arena in which the preacher first used it, the whirling world, has turned a circle or two and may have shaken everything about somewhat.

So provided it is not laziness which impels you to do it, don't be embarrassed to repeat a sermon. The second time round the congregation will probably be able to quarry fresh treasure out of the same vein of truth. Indeed, any sermon in which a preacher has invested honest effort ought to be heard again. Beethoven didn't compose his sonatas to be played once. And though we are not in that league, any painstakingly crafted sermon is still a creative act, a minor work of art. And the point about all true art is that every time we encounter it we can get more out of it than the artist put there in the first place.

Whenever I sit in the congregation and observe preachers using notes or a manuscript (and I'm certainly not arguing that they shouldn't) I'm struck by the fact that here is a preacher who has spent days or even weeks on her theme yet still needs notes to remind her of the main outline of the argument. And why not? However, it is assumed that the congregation can take it all in at one go without any visible means of support. So a second hearing may be a blessing rather than an imposition.

The sermon is a once-and-for-all event because speech is an ephemeral medium; the words which form it cannot be stopped in mid-flow and preserved. Unlike the written word, the spoken word's significance must be grasped there and then or it is lost. You may read a written sentence over and over again until you get the point. You can press the pause button of your video recorder and stop the film's flow, fixing one single image on the screen. You cannot do the same thing with a tape recorder; if you stop it you get only silence because the spoken word is an event in time whereas the written word is an object in space.

There is an immediacy about sound as a medium. If when I was a missionary in Africa I *saw* a lion in the distance lying immobile I had no way of knowing whether it was dead or alive, but if I *heard* it, then I ran. Sound is dynamic, full of movement in the way sight is not; indeed, to examine an object with our eyes we prefer that it should be still so we can get a clear look at it.

The idea of words as *symbols* is only about three thousand years old; before that, for the entire history of the human race words have been *sounds*. To put it crudely, their power was primarily in the noise they made and not the picture they conjured up in the mind. As Susan Sontag has pointed out, it is the language-line which separates human beings from the rest of the animal world. We are never more closely expressing our status as beings made in the image of God than when we speak and in so doing accomplish a minor creation. We bring something into existence, not out of nothing as God did, but certainly out of the most ephemeral of substances, our breath.

Without self-disclosure there is no true communication, and we reveal most about ourselves through the spoken word augmented by our gestures and facial expressions. Indeed, gesture is a language all of its own. Long before we could speak or understand the meaning of words we were getting our earliest knowledge of the world and of other human beings through their facial expressions and gestures. It was the Russian writer Turgenev who spoke of the 'living truth of the human face'. As I speak you can look me in the eye and judge what my words are worth, whereas when you get one of these letters from me it has no personal corroboration; you have no idea what expression was in my eyes as I penned the words. Face to face encounter through speech is the primary medium of human relationships.

An exact use of language is a skill the preacher can and must master. Unless they were note-perfect, no self-respecting violinist or pianist would dare to face an audience in a public hall. They wouldn't feel that honour was satisfied provided their fingers fell roughly in the vicinity of the correct keys or strings. Nor should any preacher expect a congregation to be indulgent about the slipshod use of words.

The literary critic Walter Pater said of the great French

novelist, Flaubert, 'He was possessed of an absolute belief that there exists but one way of expressing one thing, one word to call it by, one adjective to qualify it, one verb to animate it. He gave himself to superhuman labour in its discovery, and if the chosen word seemed not quite right, he went on seeking another with invincible patience.'[28] That is the sacred ministry of style and surely the preacher ought never to be less punctilious in exercising it than the novelist?

Think constantly in terms of the spoken word and always read with the voice. There is a natural rhythm to language used correctly. When the right words run in the right order you will have no difficulty in finding the correct places to pause or the appropriate syllables to emphasize. In every aspect of our being we live according to rhythms which for the most part pass unnoticed. It is only when we get a nail in our shoe and begin to limp or develop a stammer under stress that we realize how unconsciously rhythmic is the flow of our normal lives, including our speech.

This means that clumsiness in the use of words doesn't just undermine fluency, it also obscures meaning and forfeits the power to stir the human soul which is the sermon's primary aim. The preacher has a freedom denied to the writer, for in the interests of immediacy and directness, spoken speech may with impunity breach the rules of grammar or the laws of punctuation. Though think twice before you do it. Grammar and syntax were not invented to torment school-children. The correct way of saying something is usually also the clearest and simplest. But the speech-event may require a special use of language – which is permissible so long as the meaning is clear and the effect graceful.

By all means emulate St Ambrose in every other way but don't read your sermons with your eyes. It is the living Word that became flesh, not the manuscript.

THE USE AND ABUSE OF A TEXT

I invariably base my sermon on a biblical text because it
signals clearly what I am about – neither giving an address
nor a lecture but hopefully offering a message from God.
And that, after all, is what the congregation has the right
to expect. A text also sets boundaries to what I can say,
whereas if I pluck a subject out of thin air, the congregation
has no idea where I'm coming from, whether I'm riding
a favourite hobby horse or dealing with an issue of some
importance. And a text has the added advantage that it
serves to jog the congregation's memory. Provided I've
done my work well, after people have left the service they
may remember my text and so be able to recapitulate the
key points of the sermon.

In my early days as a preacher I was addicted to snappy
sermon titles; I recall with some embarrassment one about
the death of John the Baptist – 'He Lost His Head at a
Dance!' Because it was widely believed at the time that no
one took much notice of the Bible, it was the fashion to
keep well clear of biblical texts and preach on subjects,
Temptation, Providence, Immortality and so on. The problem was that I soon ran out of subjects because I was
attempting to compress a huge issue into a single twenty-
minute sermon. Once I reverted to preaching from biblical
texts I found I had an inexhaustible mine of rich material.
Perhaps the great Dr Alexander Whyte was the limiting
case; he preached every Sunday morning for three years on
2 Corinthians 13:14.[29]

The point from which all biblical preaching must start is
with the exploration of what the text meant to the original
writer, and what he was trying to say to his original readers.
Granted, no matter how conscientious we are in consulting

the appropriate commentaries, there are some texts whose original meaning will defeat us because the translation isn't secure or because the issues or events to which the text refers have vanished in the mists of time. But at least we must make the attempt.

Though we should treat the Bible with the respect it deserves, we must never forget that it was written by human beings in a particular language at a definite time in history and in order to respond to specific circumstances. They lived and thought and spoke in the typical categories of their age. So our point of departure must be to try to discover what message that particular bit of the Bible is concerned to get across and to whom. Fred Craddock makes the point that whenever we modern readers come across slight variations of the same story or incident in the various gospels we tend to explain away the discrepancies by claiming that no two witnesses to the same event ever give completely identical accounts of what they saw. In fact, he points out, these differences are more likely to be due to the special emphasis an ancient storyteller will give to aspects of a story in order to meet the needs of a given audience: 'Luke records a parable of Jesus concerning a feast and the guests who did not come. Matthew tells the story for his situation but it is now an allegory with historical allusions. The gospel of Thomas tells it for another situation as a morality story against the business community. The writers are carrying out their obligation to bring the words of Jesus in the tradition to bear upon the lives of their hearers.'[30]

The more we study the Bible the more it strikes us that it does not worry overmuch about harmonizing its overall message so that each part is consistent with every other about a specific topic. Some of the sayings of Jesus not only diverge from others but occasionally contradict them.

Thus, in one place the New Testament exhorts us to become as little children whilst in another it tells us sharply to grow up and stop behaving like infants. The danger here is that the preacher may be so anxious to demonstrate to the congregation that he or she is aware of these inconsistencies that the sermon degenerates into a rhapsody of finely balanced and judicious statements prefaced by 'On the one hand the Bible says this ... on the other it says that.'

Let the text make its point as sharply as its original author intended without the preacher trying to create a conceptual framework that will embrace all possible meanings – the writer was a storyteller not a philosopher. Of course we cannot leave matters there, but the starting point must be the historical meaning of the verse. Though we may go way beyond it to see what it is saying to our time, if the general drift of the sermon cannot be reconciled with the text's basic meaning then we are abusing it.

Besides trying to enter into the mind-set of the text's author it is also necessary to imagine so far as one is able the situation of the first readers, trying to fathom their needs and interests. To help us do this, modern scholarship offers a wealth of commentaries, some of them aimed specifically at those who know nothing of biblical languages. One legitimate short cut I've found invaluable is to compare different translations of the same verse or passage. The translators have already done the basic research, and the differing slant they put on the same word often starts a fertile train of thought. I am a great fan of the single translators, Weymouth, Goodspeed, Knox, Moffatt and Phillips – especially Moffatt and Phillips who bring clarity, vividness and colour to passages whose cutting edge has been blunted by overfamiliarity.

One word of warning. We want to cast fresh light on

familiar words and so must wrestle with the problem that many texts are so familiar to the congregation it could recite the words in its sleep. Hence, we are put on our mettle to find some new, startling twist to the text which will jerk our hearers into attention. It is one of the preacher's abiding temptations to desire to go down in history as the one who found something original to say about John 3:16 or some other classical text. Now, false modesty aside, it is unlikely that some pristine truth of God having lain dormant for twenty centuries has taken up residence in my mind so that I can offer my congregation a totally new interpretation of an old text. Indeed, given the sheer volume of sermons preached throughout Christian history it could be argued that any truly original sermon would be grossly heretical. Unless I want to found a new religion, it is not my business to be original. And after all, it's no great problem finding a completely new angle on a familiar landscape – all I have to do is stand on my head.

The originality I can legitimately hope to bring to a familiar text is my own unique, personal experience of the truth it attests. In choosing a text, it has been my experience that the sermons which have proved most effective are those which deal with themes capable of stirring my imagination, fascinating my intellect and challenging my will. Again and again I find I return to a subject which moves me deeply, and there is no evidence, even from those friends who are devastatingly honest in their judgment of my sermons, that the congregation tires of my revisiting the same truth. So long as I feel something intensely, some of the passion seems to communicate itself to my hearers and translates itself into close attention.

It is a matter of nice judgment just how much background scholarship the preacher should put on display in the sermon. The main purpose of preaching is not to make the congregation more familiar with the Bible, there are other forums in which that desirable end can be achieved. The imparting of information even about Holy Scripture must always be subordinate to our main aim which is to bring the congregation closer to God through Christ and through Christ to God.

If you begin your treatment of a text with a firm grasp of its original context and meaning, you will usually find your mind quite naturally makes connections between that original meaning and its present-day relevance. For the text was launched into the life of a real community which had cause to remember and treasure it. In turn, it became part of that community's preaching, embodied in its Gospel and so cannot avoid being germane to our day unless we doubt the relevance of the Gospel itself.

Professor John Knox in a book whose slender size is out of all proportion to its importance, *The Integrity of Preaching*, gives an example of three ways of preaching on the gospel story of Bartimaeus, the blind beggar who cried out as Jesus passed by, 'Jesus, Son of David, have mercy on me' (Mark 10:46). And Jesus healed him with a word. One sermon might use the incident as proof that Jesus was the Messiah. He was addressed as 'Son of David' and demonstrated by a miraculous act that the title was deserved. This would certainly be a legitimate use of the text, but can present-day hearers be convinced by an incident in the past that Jesus is the Christ? A second way of treating the text would be to demonstrate the sheer human compassion of Jesus and exhort the hearers to do likewise. But it's unlikely that the early Church remembered the story because such a worthy but mundane meaning was found in it.

A third way of treating the incident, says Professor

Knox, is not as a past event from which we can derive useful lessons but as a happening in our own history. '*We* are blind Bartimaeus, Christ calls to *us*, "What do you want me to do for you?" And it is we who answer, "Master, let me receive my sight." And in the measure of our faith we are brought out of darkness into his marvellous light.'[31]

It was surely for precisely this reason that the story was treasured by the early Church and became part of its Gospel; it spoke to their plight and it will speak to ours. The point that interests me about Dr Knox's exegesis is that there *is* more than one moral to be derived from the story. It demonstrates the sheer wealth of preaching material to be discovered in a well-chosen biblical text.

Given that the authors of the biblical books were men of their time with all the limitations this implies, there is another side to this which has a bearing on the use we make of their writings. None of us is always aware of the full significance of what we say and think. Transported by the occasion we may utter thoughts whose full significance we are unaware of. The point about all art is that the reader or viewer or listener can get more out of it than the artist put there in the first place. That's why we often look at a true work of art and say with admiration that it is a 'revelation' to us – we see an overplus of significance in it, a truth that had never struck us before. Indeed, when we call something *inspired*, the very word has a twofold significance – we mean it is of exceptional quality *and* also seems imbued with power breathed into it from outside.

Hence, we must be on the lookout when we study a text not simply for the meaning the writer originally intended but for truth that is *there* even though he could not have realized it. This is where that faculty which is central to all preaching, the imagination, comes into play. But we must be disciplined about it and not get carried away by the enthusiasm of the moment into totally fanciful interpretations which owe more to our natural inventiveness than to true inspiration. And the best safeguard here besides our personal integrity is the general drift of Scripture and of that book in particular from which we have drawn the text. Is our proposed interpretation consistent with what the Bible generally teaches us about God, Christ and his Church?

WRESTLE WITH THE BIG THEMES – EVEN THOUGH THEY THROW YOU

I think it is wise, at least to begin with, to stick to the big central themes of faith when you start to prepare a sermon. Every vocation has its special vanity and that of preaching often takes the form of seeking out such bizarre texts as will evoke from fellow preachers and congregations the puzzled but admiring cry, 'What on earth can he or she possibly make of *that*?' I've heard or read sermons on 'This is that' (Acts 2:16); 'Apes and peacocks' (1 Kings 10:22); 'God prepared a worm' (Jonah 4:7); 'The fourth river is the Euphrates' (Genesis 2:14); 'his bedstead was of iron' (Deuteronomy 3:11) and 'Rachel took the household gods and sat on them' (Genesis 31:34) – this text Dr Joseph Parker of the City Temple used for a sermon whose point was that a god who can be sat upon isn't much of a god. An indubitable truth, though only Parker could spin it out for fifty riveting minutes.

Whenever a preacher treats me to a display of homiletical ingenuity in starting from a bizarre text and arriving triumphantly at an exposition of a familiar Christian doctrine I'm always reminded of those conjurors who can waft their hands over a feather duster and turn it into a white rabbit. It is very clever, but I think the theatre rather than the pulpit is the appropriate venue for such displays. An unusual text may grab a congregation's attention and cast fresh light on a familiar theme, but the danger is always that the final impression is of the preacher's ingenuity rather than the Gospel's truth. Of course, it will be splendid if you are able to say something that is both true *and* striking but resist the urge to say striking things which are only problematically true.

Certainly, if you stick to the big themes you may have little that is original to say because you are following in the tracks of generations of preachers, some of whom left giant footprints in well-trodden ground. Don't be deterred by the fact that it's all been said before. It was Socrates who when his hearers complained he was always repeating himself replied, 'If I am asked what two and two make, what can I answer but "four"?' It can be a relief for the congregation to be reassured that indeed two and two *do* make four after scientists have been insisting they make five and politicians promise to make twenty-two out of them. It is on simple, majestic bedrock assertions that our belief in a stable moral order and a consistent God rest.

Like Jacob wrestling with the angel by the ford at the River Jabbok, grapple with the great texts even though they throw you. At the very least the text may linger as a sort of time-bomb in the congregation's mind, and if you really are defeated by it, well, your discomfiture will prove that biblical truth is not a puddle one can stride over with ease but a tempestuous, shoreless sea in which even the greatest preacher is likely to be swept off his feet.

Truly, we are pigmies following in the footsteps of giants and yet there is a certain sense in which our stature is to be measured by the grandeur of the peaks we attempt to climb rather than the altitude we manage to reach. Therefore, let's tackle the Olympian peaks and stick to the central apostolic themes which are concerned with those great verities, revelation, incarnation, redemption, resurrection and consummation.

Now at this point you might reasonably retort that it is unreasonable for me or for anyone else in Christendom to expect you to have come to a firm mind on some of the great doctrines over which generations of theologians have argued without a clear verdict emerging. You may need more time for reading and reflection. Indeed so. You are wise not to emulate the poacher's musket and go off at half-cock. I've had a sermon about the cleansing of the ten lepers (Luke 17) on the stocks for years. Its working title is 'When God Fails' and it resists all my attempts to hammer it into final shape. So I must let it lie until I know exactly what I want to say. I mustn't be like the man who said, 'Let's add your debts to mine and we'll be twice as rich', thereby inviting the congregation to add its confusion to my mental fog.

The sermon is not a device for clearing your mind nor is the pulpit a rostrum where you argue the pros and cons of an idea in front of an invited audience or try on daring thoughts for size before you decide whether they fit or not. Build up your theology in private. Don't be tempted to baffle the congregation with speculations that are half-formed, ideas you may well reject as flawed or even silly when your mood changes or your experience is greater. There's no hurry. Perhaps the Church of God has waited expectantly through long centuries for the precise truth with which you are about to startle it. Without doubt, it can possess its soul in patience for a few more weeks. Even then, we are not finished when we've sorted out our thinking and put into words some doctrinal position we have been worrying over; it is necessary then to live with it and subject it to the test of hard experience. For we are not offering our congregations an idea to tease their minds but a truth by which they can live. We do well to emulate the tactics of the Goths who used to formulate their battle plans twice, first when they were drunk so that they might not lack boldness, and again, when they were sober, that their boldness should be qualified by prudence.

There is a certain intellectual excitement in making what we feel are new discoveries in faith, but it's as well to allow our brain to cool and recover our sense of proportion before we impose them on a congregation. We would not ask people to live in a house the cement of whose foundations had not yet hardened into concrete. That was a temptation I sometimes fell into when I had a congregation in Central Africa. These were the heady *Honest to God* days of the late fifties and sixties; paperbacks offering daring new proposals about Christianity dropped through my letterbox like confetti. And so intoxicated was I with the intellectual excitement of these novel concepts that I could hardly wait for the following Sunday to share them with my congregation, who before long began to show symptoms of serious theological vertigo.

Of course, you should keep your congregation abreast of the way your mind is moving and your faith developing, but only do it once there is a flow, a fixed direction to your thoughts. The people have enough doubts of their own so don't burden them with yours, especially since yours may not be firm conclusions but transient rushes of blood to the head. Whilst you are awaiting some degree of stability in your thinking, don't pass the time producing sermons demolishing the theology of those who *have* settled convictions, especially in wings of the Church whose doctrinal position you find uncongenial. It's great fun and very exhilarating. But in truth, the congregation is likely to find these theological jousting matches exasperating. The exposure of the errors of other Christians is a luxury we cannot afford at a time when the battle-line is drawn at the single issue: do you stand for or against Christ?

I learned this lesson the hard way when as a missionary in Northern Rhodesia, I watched the martyrdom of the Church in the Congo counter-revolution in 1960. Over three hundred missionaries, mostly Roman Catholics and extreme fundamentalists, were killed. They not only bled the same way but whether they died clutching crucifixes or Schofield reference Bibles, they died for the same reason and the same Lord. When the chips were down in that tragic mess, Christians of many different doctrinal persuasions were revealed for what they were, their theological labels abandoned with the rest of their possessions. It was enough that they did a costly thing for Jesus' sake, which after all is what Christian discipleship is about. 'Why do you call me Lord and don't do the things I command?' is the stark question of Jesus which makes us squirm.

Certainly, the preacher must challenge the congregation, striking at the root of its complacency and parochialism, its blindness to the signs of the times, its timidity, petty snobberies and pharisaism; the sheer boredom and routine of much of its life. But because the people are not fools, they know where they've failed; what they look for in a preacher's sermon is the strength to get them through the coming week.

Dr Thomas Chalmers, one of the very greatest of nineteenth-century Scottish preachers, was an austere man who when asked if there was any biblical text he regretted not preaching on more frequently replied, 'Yes, "Comfort ye, comfort ye my people, saith your God.'" And Dr Joseph Parker who often thundered the judgment of God from the pulpit of the City Temple once astounded theological students by advising them, 'Preach to broken hearts!'

In our moments of deep self-awareness no one needs to tell us what a rotten mess we've made of life, what we want to know is: what hope is there for us? Well, Christianity might be described in shorthand as faith in a God who forgives sins through Jesus Christ, so the answer has got to be a resounding 'Yes, there is hope.' Paul told the church at Corinth that 'Jesus is not Yes and No: all the promises of God find their Yes in him.' Therefore never leave a congregation loaded down with guilt and failure. Echoing in its ears as it leaves the church ought not to be the grim 'Nos!' that have marred its lives but God's great 'Yes!'. John Wesley noted in his *Journal* that he often came across congregations who had given up the ghost after writhing under preaching so severe they were stunned into inactivity. There is a fine line to be drawn between prophetic denunciation and ill-tempered scolding. By all means stab a congregation into sensitivity about its sins but don't hack it to death. Russell Maltby put the issue in a terse axiom: 'For every word about sin, preach ten about the Saviour.'[32]

And whilst I'm dealing with matters of emphasis, let me warn of the danger of the preacher degenerating into a one-string fiddle player, harping on a single theme, either theological or topical, however important. It is the fullness of the Gospel which is the preacher's remit, not any particular doctrine isolated from the rest. However adept you become at playing it, a one-string fiddle cannot encompass the fully orchestrated music of the Gospel. Monotony of voice, of style and of theme are equally deadly in rendering a congregation comatose. And what goes for repetitiveness of theological ideas applies even more so to our opinions on topical issues. We all have our hobby horses and are prone to gallop them into the pulpit and flog them to death in front of an invited audience. We may have the urge to belabour the congregation about pacifism or socialism or racial equality, Thatcherism, green issues or whatever. And when yet again we announce our perennial topic we may imagine the congregation is looking furtive because we are putting it under Judgment. In fact, the only judgment operating is its conviction that we are becoming almighty bores.

IN THE BEGINNING IS THE IDEA

All the preaching textbooks quite rightly emphasize the importance of a sermon having a sound structure. Undoubtedly too many sermons are structured at the level of words rather than ideas. To exaggerate to the point of parody – having settled on a theme, the preacher jots down every mellifluous combination of phrases related to it that his mind can conjure up. He tries out an image or an illustration or a quotation, rolls it round his tongue, pronounces it good and sets it down. The result is a tapestry of purple passages linked together by pregnant pauses. This is very much like a jerry-builder lavishing all his time and attention on the design of a house's wallpaper and hoping like mad the girders which give the building shape and strength will somehow link together by act of God or good luck.

The sermon begins with a master-idea, that is its spine, and from it flows a progression of ideas which lead one after another to an irresistible conclusion. This is the end to which the sweat and blood of preaching is directed. The master-idea must have clarity so that it cannot possibly be misunderstood or lead to digressions and irrelevancies. It also has vitality, for it generates the ideas that flow from it, and these ideas should carry forward irresistibly the main thought. Like oxen hauling a load, these ideas mustn't fight amongst themselves or stampede off in all directions otherwise the result will be chaos.

It goes without saying that the controlling idea of a sermon ought to be significant in the sense that if accepted and acted upon, it will make a significant difference to our lives and destiny. If a sermon's central thought is trivial, the sermon will crumble to inconsequential dust and the congregation will have an indignant sense that its time has been wasted.

It is a quirk of mine that I take into the pulpit neither notes nor a full manuscript, so it is vital that I nail down firmly the controlling idea of the sermon and those that flow from it, for to put it at its lowest, a firm grasp of that idea is the only safety device I've got. I must be able to follow like a route map a succession of ideas so that I don't have to rely on my memory which gets more fallible as I grow older. I know my next step because if I've got the structure right there is nowhere else to go – B follows from A and C from B as night from day. Even were I to commit my sermon to writing, that skeletal structure of ideas is still necessary to shape, control and discipline prose that otherwise might get discursive.

Where do such controlling ideas come from in the first place? I tend to derive them by a process of self-interrogation in the presence of God. What do I want to say to these people? How can I put it? Is it true, and if so, what follows from it? That last question is critical. When Dr Thomas Chalmers was congratulated on a great sermon he replied impatiently, 'Yes, but what did it do? What followed?' The sermon is not a verbal stroll round some intellectual and spiritual terrain in order to admire the view; it is an urgent journey to a destination. And it is a call to action. As the sermon approaches its climax, the congregation ought to be echoing the cry of the rich young ruler, 'What then must I do?' And the preacher should tell them.

There is one vital point you must take account of in trying to decide whether your sermon structure is sound. *You* think it makes sense, the argument is watertight, its logic will withstand challenge. But it is not your judgment that matters. You can visualize the sermon's whole scheme laid out in manuscript or note form and have confidence that all the jigsaw pieces are in place to create a complete picture. The problem is that you have no way of transferring that picture in one movement into the mind of your hearers. Like all spoken speech, a sermon is a movement in time, therefore the congregation can only receive it bit by bit; it's as though having assembled your jigsaw picture at your study desk you then have to hand it out one piece at a time to the congregation and hope that it too can make a picture from it. But its task is much more formidable than yours because you have spent hours assembling the puzzle, whereas it has to put each piece into place quickly before you hand out the next one.

The structure may be sound in the preacher's estimation but does it make equal sense to the hearer? The person in the pew cannot see what you see when you look down at your notes or manuscript – he does not have the aids of capitals, punctuation, paragraph indentations or point numbers, he has only your voice, gestures and bodily movements to go on. You have assembled the sermon visually on a sheet of paper or a computer screen; those who hear it must receive it audibly, they must grasp it through their ears.

Furthermore, you've almost certainly read that sermon manuscript a dozen times, going over again and again any parts of it that were not immediately clear to you. The hearers have no such luxury. They cannot turn back a few pages, pick up the argument at an earlier stage and follow it through a second time. They've got to get the point there and then because if they lose track, you've already moved on to the next thought and what they've missed has gone for ever. What they do not grasp at the time, they will be unable to remember afterwards when the service is over and they are trying to recollect what you said.

Therefore, having evolved your structure, listen to it as though for the first time. Do you develop each step in the argument at a pace the congregation can firmly grasp before you move on to the next one? Have you avoided verbal conceits, decorative irrelevancies that distract the hearer, have you removed all rarefied words and startling images which though aesthetically satisfying to you will bring the congregation up short in bafflement? Remember the curse of St Ambrose and test your sermon structure with your ears rather than your eyes.

THE MARKS OF SOUND STRUCTURE

Let me summarize what seem to me to be the essential characteristics of a good sermon structure. First, *unity*. One theme runs through the sermon from beginning to end as straight as an arrow without digressions or irrelevancies. You mustn't wander off into any fascinating byways nor pause to toy with any secondary subject only loosely related to the main theme. If you choose to divide your subject into a number of points, be very sure that each point does not become in effect a separate homily, so that the whole sermon is just a rag-bag of thoughts tied loosely together or a collection of sermonettes joined by a single text. Just as a sculptor turns a block of marble into a statue by a process of chipping away superfluous material, so you must pare down by omitting any thought or image not strictly necessary. The acid test is this: could a man or woman in the pew tell someone who wasn't there what the sermon's central thought was in a couple of sentences?

I've already mentioned *order*, the logical sequence of ideas that follow one after another irresistibly, and I would include as a sub-division of it *balance*, the need to ensure that each thought receives as much time and stress as its importance demands, and no more. It is fatally easy to be carried away by expansive oratory in the early stages of a sermon and then end up rushing through the remaining points at an undignified gallop as time or congregational patience ebbs.

Then I would emphasize *lucidity*. Is the sermon couched in language both plain and elegant so that there are no obscurities of meaning caused either by the imprecise use of words or overindulgence in verbal ornamentation? Will the hearer be able to follow you from the first sentence to the last without effort? Lucidity is often confused with simplicity; in fact, lucidity is a quality of style whilst simplicity is a quality of thought. A sermon may or may not be simple, that depends on its subject and on the preacher's chosen method of dealing with it, but it must always be lucid. And in the end, lucid speaking is a function of clear thinking.

I think that closely allied to clarity is *beauty*. Try to make a little music when you put words together. After all, the congregation has a right to expect the very best combination of words being used for the very highest purpose. To speak carelessly in public is to declare to the world that we put little value on our thoughts. And the preacher who does that is like a costermonger who booms his wares by crying, 'Rotten Apples!' Having shared of the sermon with you ought to be an experience the congregation looks back on with satisfaction.

Then there is *movement*. The pace at which a sermon's argument moves is of critical importance. Both the human eye and the human mind are designed to follow movement. I discovered this to my cost when I preached a series of TV sermons from the chapel of the University of Sussex some years ago. Half a dozen sparrows had got into the building and swooped and soared over my head as I tried to preach, and however forcefully I spoke I was unable to prevent the eyes of the congregation from following them. Perhaps the harsh truth was that the birds were moving and my sermon wasn't. At any rate, the congregation was not being deliberately inattentive, merely demonstrating the truth that the human eye has a nervous mobility which virtually compels it to watch a moving object in preference to one that is still. The human mind also looks for movement in whatever attracts its attention.

Movement in a sermon is to some extent a question of sound structure but is equally a matter of psychology. The preacher establishes a rhythm which the congregation responds to and amplifies in the way one instrument can set off vibrations in others. The congregation does much to determine a sermon's pace by its reaction to what is being said. Its imperceptible drawing-in of breath when a thought grips it; the throat-clearing and restlessness when it's got the point and wants to move on; that uneasy silence which falls when it has to grapple with an uncongenial idea

– then like the Athenians to whom Paul spoke of the Resurrection they are signalling, 'We will hear you again on this subject.'

Only experience enables a preacher to sense the complex reactions of a congregation to what is being said. But don't worry yourself about this because congregations are very forbearing. They can be relied on to apply with love and understanding the mystical goad which keeps preachers moving or the bit that holds them back. In a word, learn to trust the congregation.

Thinking of movement, there comes a point in most sermons when the congregation, however interested in what you say, begins to falter; its attention lags. It is very hard work to concentrate on a closely argued theme expressed in words without any visual aids. So it's wise to allow for a break in tempo so that the congregation can catch its breath, metaphorically stretch its limbs and settle back for the final dash to the finishing post. One way to do this is to be absolutely honest with the people, telling them possibly by means of a humorous aside exactly what you are up to. That at least gives them a sense they are part of the preaching process and not the passive targets of pulpit oratory.

Charity is an essential quality in a sound sermon. However severely you must deal with the congregation in the light of the sermon's theme, your attitude must be free from bitterness or sarcasm. People cannot be sneered into the Kingdom of Heaven. Because the Church vests much authority in the preacher, the pulpit is ideally placed strategically as a launching pad from which to hurl thunderbolts of prophetic denunciation, shafts of biting wit and wounding judgments against those who differ from us. It's all very exhilarating and gets the adrenaline flowing but except on the very rarest of occasions, it is totally self-defeating. Of course, if the congregation truly believe you love and care for it, it will accept your sternest admonitions; if it doesn't, it'll keep its head down and await with resignation the last hymn.

Finally, there is *intensity* or passion. I content myself with repeating the point I made earlier that a theme which doesn't excite the preacher will leave the congregation unmoved. When the pianist Anton Rubenstein was performing in New York he was asked if he would like to go to church on the following Sunday. He replied, 'Yes, if you can take me to hear a preacher who will tempt me to do the impossible.' But be sure the stirring challenge to do the impossible is carried by the sermon's main theme and is not added by way of a rhetorical flourish at the end. Don't echo the Baghdad fruit vendor's cry, 'In the Name of Allah, figs!' – where the portentousness of the message's form clashes with the banality of its content.

The sermon leaves your desk as a structure of ideas and becomes an organism. Having been built, it then grows. All higher forms of life have both bone and tissue; a pulsating mass of cells as well as a skeleton. In the pulpit the framework is transformed into a living thing, words become the Word for that occasion. Remember that passage in the 37th chapter of Ezekiel where the prophet is bidden to preach to dry bones. The bones lie scattered, disorganized around him, but as he speaks, bone knits itself to bone, flesh covers the framework and finally God's spirit infuses the corpses and they stand on their feet, 'an exceeding great army' – a vision of irresistible power.

That is a parable of good sermon construction. Material, form, beauty and life come together in that sequence to create the sermon. You have gathered material upon which you impose order, structure, then it is knit into language

which has clarity and grace and finally comes to life. How?
Well, after Ezekiel has prophesied to the dry bones and seen
them transformed into lifeless corpses he is commanded to
prophesy again, this time to the four winds of heaven where
God's spirit blows freely. In answer to the preacher's
prayerful entreaty, a sermon which is still lifeless and un-
worthy of its high purpose is invigorated by the Spirit
of God.

THREE

THE PERFORMANCE

MAKING A PUBLIC EXHIBITION
OF ONESELF

The Apostle Paul told the church at Corinth that to follow
Christ is to become a *theatron*. Most versions of the New
Testament translate that Greek word as 'spectacle' but
the term's association with the London Palladium is irresistible. The preacher cannot avoid being a *theatron*, a
public spectacle, for preaching is one of the performing arts.
To this extent you are in the same business as the stand-up
comedian, the actor, the politician and the barrister.

Of course, preaching isn't *just* a performance. Preachers
are not contortionists whose skill is measured by their
capacity to tie themselves in knots in front of an invited
audience, though believe me, you will certainly do that
more often than you would wish. But preaching *is* a public
performance, and you must never forget that. You will have
to face people, look them steadily in the eye and project
yourself, for as the most famous definition of preaching,
that of Phillips Brooks, makes clear, preaching is truth
conveyed through *personality*. Though according to the
Old Testament God once spoke through the jawbone of
an ass, the pulpit is no place for mice. A preacher may be
humble or modest, but never timid. A timid preacher is like

a nervous surgeon; the patient will probably bleed to death from a dozen hesitant strokes when only an heroic incision will do.

In the New Testament, of course, preaching is referred to as proclamation – which suggests both formal and public speech, and furthermore, the Greek word indicates that proclamation is what heralds do. And heralds cannot be shrinking violets. Traditionally they have been splendidly dressed to draw attention to themselves, to ensure that they stood out in the crowd, for if they weren't public spectacles no one would notice them and so they couldn't get their message across.

Now, I can understand why self-projection is anathema to you because it so easily shades into spiritual exhibitionism and pride and we have all been taught that such vices ought to have no foothold in the Christian life. It is a proper humility that makes you wish to shrink into invisibility and become a still small voice rising gently from behind the pulpit Bible. But unless you present yourself boldly, visibly and audibly before the congregation *and perform* there can be no preaching.

All public performers must be entertainers in the sense that they can interest, create expectancy and hold the attention of their hearers. People may be cured by a drug they have no faith in or earn a good living in a job they dislike or be benefited by a Government they voted against but they cannot be moved by a sermon which does not interest them. If you are unable to entertain a congregation you will find it impossible either to instruct or inspire it. And you will certainly not change it, and that's what it's all about.

St Augustine, quoting the great classical orator Cicero, said that a sermon should instruct, delight and convince its hearers. Of these three essential qualities perhaps the most surprising is the admonition that we should *delight* our congregations. To delight is to please greatly; and that is what the public performer does – he or she occupies the audience's mind agreeably; makes the sermon a satisfying experience for the listeners. All true entertainment is intended to have a tonic or recreational effect, to replenish rather than deplete life-energy, to be a cordial for drooping spirits, even when its theme is sombre. Certainly, a sermon may cut its hearers to the quick but if it leaves no room for hope then it has failed not only as Gospel but also as entertainment.

I beg you, do not underestimate the importance of preaching as genuine entertainment. After all, in Victorian and Edwardian times, the public queued for hours to hear great preachers who offered them a virtuoso performance much like that of a music hall star, though their purpose, of course, was much more serious. Granted, there are outstanding preachers whose style is the very antithesis of public performance. They read their sermons, barely lifting their eyes from the manuscript, standing immobile, totally without gestures or facial mannerisms. And yet such is the quality of their thought, the beauty of their voice and the graciousness of their presence that congregations hang on every word. Thomas Chalmers, generally agreed to be one of the very greatest of Scottish preachers, followed his manuscript with his finger, line by line, his other hand beating time to the rhythm of his speaking, looking up at the congregation only occasionally. But, then, genius makes its own rules.

If by the providence of God your preaching style turns out in the end to make few concessions to public performance, so be it. But it's risky to cultivate at the outset such a paradoxical skill, the understated presentation which in the acting profession occasionally wins an Oscar. That glazed expression in the congregation's eyes *might* mean it is entranced by your refusal to descend to the vulgar skills of the performing artist, but I wouldn't bank on it.

Many outstanding exponents of the public arts are not natural performers and are shaken by stage fright every time they appear in public. Indeed, some artists claim it is this inner turmoil which drives necessary adrenaline round their system. You may never completely conquer pulpit nerves; many preachers don't. But it's just possible that there may come a point when sadly you realize beyond a shadow of a doubt that your inner anguish when facing the public is exacting too high a price from you in happiness, health and spiritual serenity. This doesn't mean you've misheard God's call but that you've not yet precisely located the sphere where you can best exercise it. The Church offers many forums in which you can testify to the faith that is in you, but perhaps the pulpit is not one of them.

It isn't just for your own sake that you should count the cost of public performance, there is also the congregation to consider. Nothing is more unsettling to the people in the pews than the sight of a preacher struggling with crippling stage fright. And they will probably be so distressed at your discomfiture that they don't hear a single word you say. When Paul wrote about the follower of Christ becoming a *theatron*, he particularly had in mind the dumb beast that was dragged into the arena to be humiliated for the pleasure of the crowd. Decent people find equally distressing the spectacle of a dumb animal's suffering or the inner torment of a preacher temperamentally ill-matched to his or her vocation. Believe me, I'm really not trying to discourage you. But whether one sets out to build a tower or become a preacher it is as well to count the cost.

There was a great early nineteenth-century Scottish

preacher, Guthrie of Linlithan, who was ejected from his pulpit during a period of church-state turmoil. He was replaced by an Episcopalian parson who was a poor preacher, though Guthrie in a great act of grace was content to sit in his old congregation and went faithfully each week to hear the new minister. One Sunday Guthrie was returning from the service across the moors accompanied by a number of the congregation who were complaining bitterly about the poor quality of the sermon they'd just heard. Guthrie disagreed and said it had been excellent, and to prove his point, stood on a tree stump and proceeded to preach the sermon using the same points and illustrations. The hearers were stunned; it was the same sermon and yet utterly transformed. Guthrie brought to it that indefinable something which makes the born preacher.[33]

There are many aspects of preaching that can be taught but not *that* – you've either got it or you haven't. And you'll soon find out! Since this is a factor quite outside your control, I mention it only to urge you not to despair when you listen to preachers who undoubtedly have a kind of native genius. They are a tiny elite; the main burden of preaching the Word week in and week out is carried on by workmanlike preachers who demonstrate competence rather than virtuosity which, judging by the results, God finds quite acceptable.

In a way, preaching is like one of those tag-wrestling matches where you face two opponents, both of whom must be dominated and subdued – your chosen theme and the congregation's fitful attention-span. And not every Christian has or need have the stomach for such public combat. Pursue that fight image a little further. There is a sporting term which is now used much more widely of any virtuoso performance – 'He or she rang the bell!' We mean they hit the target, stunned the audience, scored a palpable triumph. It could have a higher meaning. At the critical point of the Catholic Mass when the host is elevated, a bell is rung to signify the unequivocal presence of God in Christ. I hope that is one bell you will always ring.

TAKING RISKS

As we have seen, preaching is one of the performing arts and therefore we have much to learn by studying the technique of other professional performers. I have been taught much by observing the technique of stand-up comedians. I'm sure there are those who will reject any analogy between light entertainment and preaching, insisting that the context of worship is, because of the presence of the Holy Spirit, unique and totally set apart from any secular activity. I respect that view but I do not share it. A congregation doesn't live in a vacuum-sealed bubble all week; it is exposed to dozens of entertainment programmes on television which inevitably school it to recognize a certain level of professionalism in public performance. Psychologically, people cannot suddenly switch into a different gear on Sundays and tell themselves that this person standing in front of them must not be judged by the normal standards of public performance.

When I worked in the BBC I had dealings with some of the great comedians of our time and I learned just what a hazardous business it is standing alone in front of a large audience and trying to make them laugh. The late Les Dawson said that he felt the loneliest man on earth when marooned in a pool of light on a stage facing an audience daring him to amuse them. Professional performers talk about 'dying' on stage when they are unable to win control of the audience and instead of approval are met with restlessness and half-hearted laughter. By all accounts, it is a harrowing experience, but if there is to be that electric interaction between performer and audience risks have got to be taken.

All forms of public performance require this willingness to take risks. The relationship between performer and audience is a living, unpredictable thing; the joke that brings the house down one night drops to the floor and shatters like a pane of glass the next. But the performer, whether preacher or stand-up comedian, must be prepared to become vulnerable in order to establish rapport with audience or congregation. It is this frisson of danger which generates the electricity that sparks the listeners into life.

What sort of risks ought the preacher to take? I recently watched a religious TV Christmas programme which featured Cliff Richard and other pop stars. They danced and sang their lyrics from memory. Then the parson came on to tell the Christmas story and there he was, at the end of every sentence, looking down at copious notes. Why? He had told that story a thousand times before. If Cliff Richard had come on stage waving a manuscript which he consulted before each stanza of the songs he was singing, he would have been booed off stage. So why did the parson behave in such a way as to undermine the rapport all the other performers had struggled to establish between themselves and the audience?

Some might retort that this was a television show and there were millions of people watching whereas that parson was probably used to addressing the proverbial baker's dozen. That may be true, but when the parson agreed to appear on the show he knew what he was in for. And after all, what was the worst that could happen? He might dry up or stumble over his words. He would soon recover; it's amazing how resilient public performers are at finding words to talk themselves out of a tight spot. And we are talking about a professional; a clergyman is paid for doing a number of things, one of which is to stand up in public and speak.

When I was the BBC's Head of Religious Television, I recall attending a *Songs of Praise* recording where the Blessing was to be delivered by the local Bishop. At the rehearsal he produced a script and I asked him what was on it. 'The Blessing,' he said. 'But surely', I said, 'you must have said the Blessing a dozen times this week.' 'Ah,' he said, 'but not on television, supposing I were to dry up?' Supposing he did. What would it prove other than the fact that he was human and fallible and capable of falling flat on his face like the rest of us?

All this raises the Notes versus No Notes argument. Let me run quickly through the five possible ways of delivering sermons. You may write your sermon out, word for word, and read it with more or less freedom. But unless it is well done, the result is still *reading* rather than *preaching*. You may write your sermon out, memorize it and then recite it. In the old-fashioned preaching books this is known as *mandating* and it is the worst possible method. A sermon which is being recited is still a read sermon except that it is being read from the back of your head rather than from a manuscript. Then again, you may write the sermon out fully, master it and then speak from summary notes. Or you may work the sermon structure out fully in your mind and then regurgitate it on your feet, relying on your vocabulary to find the appropriate words in which to clothe it. There is also a fifth possibility, preaching *ex tempore* – the Latin phrase means 'on the spur of the moment', speaking without any prior preparation, trusting in a ready wit and native fluency to get you by. Some preachers who use this method clothe themselves in the dubious authority of Jesus' words for a quite different set of circumstances, 'Take no thought for what you will say; the Holy Spirit will give you utterance.'

Let's forget the *ex tempore* method which is strictly for garrulous bores or giants of the Church such as St Augustine who often prepared one sermon and then was seized by some words in the Scriptures which were read before the sermon so he preached on them instead. But then he was a great theologian with a mind bursting with sacred knowledge who spent hours every day studying the Bible. Whatever the appointed Lessons, he would be on familiar ground and so never unprepared. For the rest of us, and especially for apprentice preachers, those methods are best which require a sermon being fully written out first. Francis Bacon said that writing makes an 'exact man'. There is a necessary discipline in finding the best possible combination of words to clothe the most exactly worked out thoughts. It *is* drudgery, but without it we are always in danger of becoming sloppy in both speech and thought, and because we all have our favourite expressions, we soon begin to think and talk in well-worn grooves.

Once we have mastered the manuscript, then we decide which form of delivery is most congenial to us and that is often a matter more of temperament and training than anything else. I would only warn you that it takes much greater skill to read powerfully and naturally than to speak well without notes and you always have the problem of trying to maintain eye-contact with the congregation without losing your place.

As for memorizing your sermon, there is little to be said in favour other than the fact that it offers a spurious impression of freedom and fluency. And it *is* spurious, for behind a façade of confidence the preacher is battling against outside distractions and inward tiredness and living always in fear of his or her mind going blank. Of course, it will work if you preach only very occasionally before different congregations, for in that case, constant repetition drills the sermon into your memory. But it is a performance such as an actor delivers after learning his lines, and does not allow for any bursts of spontaneous inspiration.

I suppose the majority of preachers favour the method of writing out their sermons in full and then taking notes into the pulpit with them. This provides a combination of discipline through writing and freedom in speaking. The odds are that this is the style you are likely to settle on, though it is not a discipline I have ever been able to master because I suffer from the psychological quirk that if I once break eye-contact with the congregation and look down at notes or a manuscript I'm lost; I just dry up. So by long experience I've evolved a method which requires me to work out the sermon structure in my head and then rely on the occasion to furnish the words. It's a risky business and whilst it has the virtue that I can address the congregation directly, I am at the mercy of my physical and mental condition. Should I be really tired it takes me much longer to say what I have to say than would be the case if I were on top form. I especially find it hard to bring the sermon to a climax; like a pilot who's lost his bearings I meander round and round looking for a place to land. The salutary discipline of notes does encourage brevity rather than expansiveness, for which the congregation at least will be grateful.

But whichever method you settle on, I would beg you

to take more risks than many preachers feel is wise. If your sermon really possesses you, if it has mastered your mind and kindled your imagination, if the structure is sound, its points marching forward in an irresistible logical progression, then trust yourself to take wings and fly, at first with your notes on the pulpit lectern as a safety net, but then, leave them behind and rely on the Holy Spirit to endorse the careful preparation you have made. It is quite possible you may find the experience so scarifying that you resolve never to do it again. So be it. You have discovered the limits of the possible for you; you can refine your chosen method with a quiet mind.

I would add only this. If you use notes, learn to handle them with such freedom that it seems you are preaching *ex tempore*; if you preach without notes or manuscript, let your speech be so disciplined that it seems you are speaking from a full manuscript.

But whatever your method of delivery you must be prepared for the totally unexpected when you stand before a congregation. There may come a moment in the pulpit when you have an overwhelming conviction, you really know deep in your heart, that you must tear up your manuscript because you have prepared the right sermon for the wrong occasion. You must have the courage to scrap it and rely on God to haul you out of the yawning chasm that faces you, and if that is what you determine to do, it's wise to confide in the congregation. It will approve your concern to speak a relevant word to their situation, applaud your courage and cheer you on. The result will probably not be elegant, because spontaneous speech rarely is, but it's the aim not the decorativeness that matters.

When you find yourself facing such a crunch, all the shelves of textbooks, the piles of concordances will be of little use to you, and you will have to speak not out of your head but from the heart. That has happened to me, and it may well happen to you. But be of good cheer. Once it has happened to you, you will never be overly nervous about preaching again because you will have found out that God is to be trusted.

ON TIMING AND TIME

Another important lesson I've learned by watching and listening to other professional performers such as comedians is the importance of timing. I watched a rerun of one of the late Tommy Cooper's routines on TV the other evening. He comes on carrying an oil painting and a violin announces that he's got there a Stradivarius and a Rembrandt. 'There's a problem,' he says, holding up the painting – 'Stradivarius was a lousy painter', then he picks up the violin and waits as the audience gets the point and begins to laugh. Then without another word he breaks the violin across his knee, and the place erupts. But the point is that had he done it twenty seconds earlier or later most of the impact would have been lost. The real star has a superb sense of timing; he or she knows just how long to spin out the dramatic tension before resolving it.

What's this got to do with preaching? Everything, I think. I listened a few weeks ago to a young preacher who in my opinion will do great things for God. He had thought out his sermon with great care, he phrased it beautifully, chose illustrations that were apt and moving and then totally undermined them by his inability to deliver the pay-off line correctly. He either moved on so quickly that the congregation didn't have time to grasp the full import of what he was saying or spun out the tension until people lost the point. Faulty timing in delivery undermines hours of careful preparation.

To some extent, correct timing is a matter of experience but you can augment it by listening carefully to professional raconteurs such as comedians and study the way they tell stories and play the audience like a well-tuned instrument. We preachers have much to learn about public performance and we cannot afford to be too choosy where our models come from. There are thousands of comedians performing at any one time and according to one student of comedy only about seven variations on the standard joke, so the difference between stars and the rest is more likely to be a matter of timing than anything else.

One cause of faulty timing in a public performer is incorrect breathing. When we breathe from the upper chest rather than the diaphragm we find ourselves running out of breath before we reach the end of a longish sentence and so begin to rush. In this way the timing of what we say is falsely determined not by the dramatic requirements of the text but by shortage of breath. My point is easily demonstrated. First take a deep breath and breathe out emptying the upper chest, then holding the chest still, breathe out from the belly and continue to exhale until you reach the point of giddiness. You may be surprised at the volume of air available to you which normally remains unused. There are no more worthwhile and practical aids to preaching than simple breathing exercises. They can transform your whole delivery in timing, pitch, emphasis and audibility.

But there is another form of timing besides speed of delivery which the preacher must wrestle with – the duration of the sermon. I can tell you exactly how you can go about the business of being the most popular preacher in the area – just keep your sermons shorter than anyone else's and you will be almost universally applauded. But not by me. Call me an ecclesiastical dinosaur but I feel cheated when I sit in the pew and I'm treated to a very short sermon.

I've come to church with matters of some moment on my mind and conscience and I'm eager to know what God's word has to offer me by way of judgment and renewal; I just don't believe God speaks in the pulpit equivalent of Christmas cracker mottos. If I want a ten-minute cheery chat interspersed with music I can stay in bed, turn on the radio and listen to my favourite disc jockey. If I had to have an operation, I doubt I would say to the surgeon, 'Only one thing matters, keep the operation short.' After all, he could amputate a badly injured limb in a few minutes whereas it would take much longer to repair it. But who in his right mind would begrudge the extra time?

The essayist and novelist Charles Morgan commenting as a layman on reasons why increasing numbers of people stay away from worship wrote, 'The most frequent disappointment is in the sermons – not, as many parsons modestly suppose, because they are too long, or because they give offence, but for the opposite reason, that they are too scanty, that they do not strike deep enough.'[34]

Obviously I'm not arguing that a sermon's quality is invariably in direct proportion to its length. I *am* suggesting that by definition the preacher has undertaken to deal with matters of eternal significance and the members of the congregation are entitled to hear the argument spelled out at whatever length is necessary for them to grasp it. As a preacher you will have wrestled with your theme for days or possibly weeks, and if it is of any importance, the congregation can hardly be expected to grasp it in a few minutes – not unless you are a theological and pulpit genius

like the late Austin Farrer who preached ten-minute sermons that were simple, profound and beautiful expositions
of his theme. If so, you don't need my help.

As you know well, the people in the pews don't exist in a
vacuum from Sunday to Sunday; they are preoccupied by a
thousand and one problems of daily living. They need time
to clear their minds of irrelevancies and get their thinking onto the same wavelength as your own. Systematic
thought, the following through of an argument, is hard
work, especially for those whose everyday business is quite
different. Hence, don't omit steps in the argument or gallop
through complexities out of the mistaken belief that in
shortening the sermon you are sparing the congregation
grief; all you are doing is denying it understanding.

Of course there will always be members of the congregation who signify their impatience and restlessness if you are
not as brief as they feel you ought to be. Such faint-hearts
missed a treat in not being exposed to the formidable Dr
R.W. Dale of Carr's Lane, Birmingham who on one occasion having preached for fifty minutes said, 'I hope I have
disposed of some of your preliminary queries concerning
this text, so I shall now move on to my first main point . . .'

You must try to raise the attentiveness of restive hearers
to your level, at all costs you mustn't sink to theirs, otherwise every member of the congregation will be penalized as
a result. I fully concede there are times when had I put twice
as much effort into the preparation of a sermon I could
have said it all in half the time. It's often idleness that makes
us aggregate every thought we've had about a subject and
lay it out at length in order to be sure we don't miss anything essential. It goes without saying that we mustn't
trespass on the congregation's patience, but we shouldn't
underestimate its purposefulness either.

It takes two to make a bargain. Congregations need to be reminded that it is their interest or lack of it which makes a sermon seem long or short. The best way for members of a congregation who find sermons a trial to sail through one, is to listen to it with close attention. If they only listen now and then between periods of reverie, the sermon is bound to sound tedious, for their perception of duration has ceased to be a matter of elapsed time and become a function of their concentration span.

One eminent American preacher I know always advises theological students to avoid using in their sermons any expressions which hint at the passing of time – pointers such as 'first', 'secondly' or 'finally'. He insisted that the preacher should under no circumstances concede that he or she is trying the congregation's patience or demanding from it heroic concentration. One of his party pieces is to demonstrate dramatically how intolerably slowly time passes when our attention is drawn to it. He would strike a note on a piano, time the interval by his watch and then strike a second note, inviting the audience to guess the duration of the interval. Most greatly overestimated the time-lapse.

We preachers must always remember that divine worship isn't the only claim on people's time. There are many diverting ways to spend a couple of hours on Sunday, so we are entitled to assume that the congregation is in church because it means business. Hence, we should make the sermon as concise as is consistent with tackling the theme properly. For in the end, elapsed time according to the clock is irrelevant; what matters is duration, the congregation's *sense* of time. Like you, I've listened to some preachers for forty minutes and the time went by in a flash; other preachers can make ten minutes seem like an eternity.

Thoughtful people will stay with us for as long as it takes when they realize that what we have to say is important.

LISTEN, THEN SPEAK

When I was a student in theological college we were honoured by a visit from one of the most popular preachers of the day, and a group of us were delegated to entertain him, show him round the college, give him tea and then take him off to his evening engagement in one of the central churches in the city. It was a bone-wearying experience. The great man got out of his car talking, he talked solidly throughout the afternoon, barely noticing his surroundings and certainly not pausing long enough to ask us our names, he talked through tea and throughout the car journey into the city. It was riveting stuff for he was a natural storyteller, witty, eloquent, self-deprecating. His comments on the state of the Church, the foibles of its leaders, the weaknesses of modern theology were trenchant. Yet we rated his visit an utter disaster because he treated us not as people but as a captive audience. He asked not a single question and evinced no curiosity about us or our environment – like a mighty wind he blew in, through and out of our lives, sweeping aside everything and everyone in his path. And his sermon that evening demonstrated the same abstraction: it was a superb exhibition of oratory, packed with interesting ideas and daring proposals, but it was anchored firmly in mid-air. He was so remote he could well have arrived from another planet, there was no evidence that any human encounter had made an impact upon him. A preacher without curiosity about other human beings is like a colour-blind painter or tone-deaf musician.

I regale you with this account of an exasperating after-noon simply to make the point that one of the essential qualifications of the true preacher is the ability to listen as well as to speak; indeed, preaching is a listening vocation. He or she hears and overhears countless everyday conver-sations, the cries of triumph and tragedy, of suffering and outrage in news bulletins, the prating of politicians, the prognostications of economic pundits, the gossip of show business and high society, the roar of the sports crowd and the beat of popular songs. Then there are those voices deep within us, articulating our own pain and hopes and fears. These voices are a veritable Babel; they certainly do not speak in unison, yet just as God brought order out of chaos at the Creation so the preacher is challenged to distil from them the raw material of sermonizing.

There are voices to which the preacher must attend with close attention. There are the sermons the Bible preaches to us. We usually bring to bear upon the sacred text all the resources of modern scholarship, but there are times when the one thing needful is not to dissect the text but to sit down like a little child before a biblical passage and listen to it without any attempt at sophisticated analysis. Even those parts of the Bible that I can't read as I would have done had Galileo, Darwin and Einstein never existed – Genesis 1 and 2 for example – I can still receive as *proclamation* rather than *information* – not 'This is how the Creation came about', but, 'This is God declaring that he is the ground and source of all being'. We must just receive the full force of what the Bible is saying to us at that moment.

Then there is the voice of the congregation. I am not suggesting that we should stand around eavesdropping in order to garner homiletical illustrations or use fellow Christians as sermon-fodder. Yet the preacher does not just preach *to* a congregation but *out* of it, out of the plenitude of its on-going life; all the mess and confusion of it, its inevitable routines and occasional flashes of glory. For what the preacher dare never forget is that the Church is prior to all else in Christianity. There is a popular misconception of the history of Christianity which suggests that groups of early Christians having read the gospel accounts of Jesus decided to form themselves into congregations at Rome and Corinth and Ephesus rather as supporters of Elvis Presley establish themselves in fan clubs. In fact, the precise opposite is the case. The Church did not come out of those accounts of Jesus' life we call the gospels; the gospels came out of the Church. They didn't establish the Church; the Church wrote them. What we call the Gospel is the Church preaching; theology is the Church thinking, worship is the Church addressing and being addressed by God; the New Testament is the Church remembering, mission is the Church helping God to enlarge the frontiers of the Kingdom of Heaven, the sacraments are the Church continuing the drama of the Incarnation.

We sometimes talk about the Church in general as though it were a kind of ideal of which local churches are a partial and imperfect reflection. But the Church in general is an abstraction found in theological textbooks and on legal documents. There is no other Church than the local church. That's what Incarnation means. The essence of Incarnation is locality. You can't be incarnate in general, you are incarnate in a particular place or nowhere. Where the church exists at all, it exists in its entirety. If the One, Holy, Catholic and Apostolic Church is not to be found at St Gertrude's by the Gasworks, it is not to be found anywhere. All the authority and power and duties of the great historic Church fall to that baker's dozen who week by week are dotted amongst its pews; and the great Church's privileges are theirs too.

Hence, the preacher must listen to the Church; not just to its national leaders and official pronouncements but to local gossip and plans and programmes and events, for in all that is the seed-bed of the contemporary Church's faith.

And the preacher must listen to the world. We Western Christians are much better at giving than receiving, at teaching than learning. The historical arrogance of power has robbed us of humility. I know whereof I speak. I spent sixteen years as a missionary in Africa; I brought back with me more of the faith than I took out; I learned more than I taught, received more than I gave. I came to recognize that the traditional African in the tiny village occupies a thought-world much more extensive than that of the average Western city dweller. I was privileged to share a rich culture enlivened by human qualities we in the West have lost or never had. The African people received the Gospel I took with me and by bringing their peculiar genius to bear on it, handed it back to me an immeasurably greater thing.

And I have not ceased to learn since I left Africa. A Buddhist monk in Vietnam taught me what the burning charity of Christ might look like in action; an avowed atheist philosopher always comes to mind when I think of that quality of integrity-on-fire Jesus according to John's Gospel called 'doing the truth'; the Muslim's fierce defence of God's honour has been a reproach to my rather limp reverence; and when I was writing a book about religious humour, those Jewish sages, the Hasidim, added an entirely new dimension to my understanding of a Laughing God. There is a gospel the world outside Christianity has to teach the Church, and the preacher must listen attentively for its distinctive notes.

So we must listen to many voices, mentally arguing with them, endorsing some and rejecting others. It won't necessarily be the first or last or loudest voice we hear that determines our sermon theme. Of course, there is more to preaching than careful listening, but before we speak we must be sure we have taken the trouble to hear. Writes David Schlaffer: 'The speaking of a sermon arises from listening to all kinds of voices. It is relatively easy for those in the pew to recognize the difference between a preacher who is constantly listening, broadly and deeply, and one who listens, if at all, only to his own voice. In and through, beneath and beyond these voices, preachers are listening for the voice of God. But the God whom the preacher is attempting to hear is not simply a talking God. We worship a God who listens as well, "I have heard the cry of my people in Egypt," God tells Moses.'[35]

SILENT COMMUNICATION

Let me say some more about listening. I used to think the term 'silent communication' was a contradiction in terms until my computer went on the blink the other day and I lost all my punctuation marks – full stops, semi-colons, capitals, the lot. All I had was endless chunks of text, great streams of words, and I suddenly realized how important silence is in communication. For that's what punctuation marks are. They are symbols of silence; where you pause, hesitate, ponder, take a breath.

All great artists are masters at speaking through silence – the object left out of the picture just where you'd expect it to be; the void in architecture, the caesura, that pause in the middle of a line of verse; the note withheld in music.

Recall, for instance, those four thundering Hallelujahs at the climax of the Hallelujah Chorus – three of them, and then a pause that seems to last for ever, and then the crashing fourth. And in the throbbing silence is an unspoken Hallelujah as piercing as the others.

Most of the profound things that happen to us happen in silence. In silence we love, in silence we pray; in silence, we worry and wait and despair. I once heard a German Christian talking about being at a bus stop in 1937 when the Gestapo came along and took a Jew out of the queue behind her and made him stand on his own. Someone asked, 'What did you do?' She replied, 'I didn't know what to do, so I just went and stood by him silently.' Now you could preach a dozen sermons against anti-Semitism and not reach that level of eloquence. Silent communication.

But how do we know it's the silence of communication? Suppose heaven is silent because it is empty? Well, in everyday life you know the difference between dead and living silences. You go into a restaurant and see two couples at adjacent tables and both are silent, but there is all the difference in the world between the two forms of silence. In one case the silence is a void, and in the other it is filled with presence. In one case, they are silent because they have nothing left to say and in the other they are silent because they have passed beyond the need for words. You know the difference between living and dead silence, because unless you've been amazingly lucky in your relationships you've been there.

Has it ever struck you how tight-lipped Jesus was? Here he was, a professional preacher and teacher – you would expect his collected works to be huge and fat like those of his distinguished rabbinical predecessors. Instead we have wafer-thin pamphlets called Gospels. Whatever Jesus did, he didn't nag people into the Kingdom of Heaven. 'Poor talkative little Christianity,' sneered E. M. Forster. Maybe, but it didn't get the habit from its founder. His most powerful messages were wordless. He kept silent about his mission for thirty years; to this very day, no scholars are sure whether he did or did not claim to be the Messiah – 'Are you he that should come or do we wait for another?' the disciples of John asked him and his answer was equivocal; he rarely answered a direct question and his response to many incidents was silence. When he was told that John had been murdered he said nothing but went into the desert; when the Syrophenician woman asked him to heal her daughter he didn't reply; and when the woman taken in adultery was brought to him the midst of a great clamour, he said nothing and wrote in the sand. He made no attempt to defend himself before Caiaphas or Herod or Pilate. He exasperated them by his silences.

And in the most momentous act of all, on Calvary, when the redemption of the world was accomplished, he spoke just seven times. And even heaven was silent then. According to the book of Revelation, as the drama of our redemption reached its climax, 'There was silence in heaven for a space.' It's as though all heaven and earth held its breath to see whether this deed would be done. St John of the Cross said that throughout eternity God has spoken only one word and that word is Jesus his Son.

What has this to do with preaching? Well, it is vital the preacher understands the nature of silence as an essential element in the communication process. And this doesn't come easily to us because we are by nature inveterate talkers. And one reason we find silence unbearable is that when we stop talking we *hear* ourselves; all the groanings of our inner dis-ease like the ominous creaking of a ship's

110

bulkheads in a storm – grinding teeth, tapping fingers, the twanging of stretched nerves. We are not at peace, so we drown out our inner dissonance with a torrent of words. What we call communication is often a form of camouflage, hiding our self-preoccupation and lack of wholeness. I guess a preacher's ability to come to terms with silence is one indicator of his or her spiritual condition.

How does silence figure in our pulpit technique? I'm not now thinking of dramatic pauses consciously contrived which may have their effect so long as they are used sparingly, otherwise the congregation will begin to suspect they are listening not to a preacher of great power but to one with a poor memory. The relationship between words and silence is threefold.

There is the silence *before* words. Some preachers gallop into the pulpit, whip out their notes and launch into their theme with barely a glance in the direction of the congregation. True silence before speech has certain parallels in the counselling situation. Doctors, for instance, who have some degree of insight into the human personality, recognize the importance of listening with close attention to a patient's rambling recital of symptoms, sometimes outward signs of an inner turmoil which is not physical in origin. And the patient may leave without a prescription but in some strange way feeling better. He or she has been heard; their personhood has been acknowledged.

Granted, the preacher's context is different since he is the one about to do the talking. But the basic principle is the same. The ministry of the Word ought to be preceded by the ministry of listening. The sounds may be vague and unrelated, shuffling, the odd cough, the noise of passing traffic and so on. These apparent irrelevances can tell the preacher much, not only about the mood and atmosphere of the congregation but the possible sources of distraction.

It is the totality of what you hear and say that determines the rhythm and style of your preaching. In a moment of silence, of keen listening, you are consciously acknowledging the personhood of every member of the congregation. They are not souls with ears into which is poured saving truth like a constant stream of tea from an urn across which a moving belt of empty cups passes. The preacher who does not know how to listen forfeits the right and ability to speak.

Sacramental silence is a good way of describing this joining of speaker and hearers in one continuum before the formal sermon begins. Both preacher and congregation are demonstrating their openness to the Holy Spirit. As the Psalmist put it, 'For God alone, my soul awaits in silence.' And some present who do not find God in the wind, earthquake and fire of a spirited sermon may hear him in that still, small voice, too subdued to break the silence which precedes our words.

Then there is the silence *between* words; and I'm not now thinking of the pace at which the preacher delivers the sermon. Silence between words acknowledges that the sermon is a living organism, growing rather than being built. In ordinary conversation, silence between words is a gesture of respect, a symbol that the one who speaks takes seriously the concerns of the hearer. By painfully struggling to find the exact word, the speaker is, in that endless moment whilst he ransacks his vocabulary, engaged in the search for a common experience which lies deeper than the level of language.

Obviously, the preacher who is tied to a verbatim manuscript has a particular problem. He has already constructed his sentences and though he may vary the speed of his delivery, his freedom to digress from the script is severely limited, if only because any passages added on the spur of the moment might distort the shape of the sermon and send him off at a tangent. Whether he uses notes, full manuscript or speaks extemporaneously, the preacher, in the silence between words, must be prepared to respond to an inner voice and utter what is in his heart rather than on his manuscript. Otherwise he may as well hand out to the congregation duplicated copies of his sermon; it is fixed, final and impervious to the subtle pressures of the Spirit on him.

Of course, there are no words for our deepest experiences, for in attempting to articulate, we trivialize. Nevertheless, silence between words demonstrates the preacher's awareness that he or she is struggling with the inexpressible; it is allowing room for mystery to break out of its linguistic prison. I know this sounds rarified, but the next time you sit in the pew and hear a sermon, listen for the difference between a genuine silence as the preacher wrestles with a profound truth, and a mere pause, a gap between bursts of God-gossip.

Silence *beyond* words is closely related to silence *between* words but it is not to be found in the sermon itself so much as in the preacher's own awareness of the consistency or lack of it between what he professes publicly and practises privately. When we proclaim what we do not believe or use oratorical tricks in order to play upon a congregation's emotions, that silence beyond words is filled with self-mocking disparagement; it's the echo of our conscience judging us. On the other hand, it may be the silence of divine approval, the way in which the third party to the preaching process signals his endorsement.

The silence beyond words embodies God's judgment on our efforts. And our ears become more attuned to its nuances the longer we practise the preacher's art. It is a verdict more absolute than the plaudits the congregation may heap upon us at the church door after the service. If we have been faithful servants of the Word that silence constitutes our inner peace; if not, it is the hollowness of dereliction.

WE, THE PREACHER

The word 'liturgy' means the work of the people, so the onus of making God real does not rest solely on the preacher but with the whole worshipping community. Indeed, we reveal the dimensions of the God we believe in by our attitude to worship. A concern for trivialities, vacancy of mind, restlessness of body, unhealthy concentration on other worshippers, half-hearted or insensitive hymn singing, fitful attention to the reading of the Scripture, clock-watching during the sermon – these are not just understandable human foibles. They spell out the vague and pathetic deity we really believe in and lead the discerning enquirer to wonder whether our God is worth worshipping.

The liturgy is both the word which the ordered Christian community addresses to its Lord and his Word to the world mediated through the Church. And it is the complete answer to pulpit subjectivity. Whatever damage we preachers may do, the liturgy can correct. Where we are churchy, the liturgy elevates the concerns of the world, when we harp on our pet themes with monotonous regularity, the liturgy deploys the whole range of Christian truth in creed and hymnody and Scripture lessons. Because it is so easy for us to preach ourselves empty, there are times when the congregation would leave undernourished were it not for the sustenance the various elements in the liturgy offer them. Whilst we have been busy darkening counsel in the pulpit, Christ has been preached in the rest of the service, and especially in the hymns.

It puts us in our place as preachers to realize this – that the deep-down faith of the congregation is more likely to be articulated in the hymns than in our sermon, for they are the essence of the pew dwellers' religion. They are an expression of democracy at the heart of religious authority. In many aspects of religion it is the professional, the priest or minister or even the choirmaster who rules the roost, by virtue of authority or knowledge or power. But the hymn book is the place where the congregation strikes back. Here is the firmest proof of that venerable doctrine, the Priesthood of all Believers. Lay people may not be able to choose the cardinal doctrines of their faith – the charismatic leaders and sacred conclaves do that – but they *can* decide what popular expressions of their faith will prevail. They vote not with their feet but with their voices. Their stubborn insistence on cherishing some hymns and studiously neglecting others decides the shape and content of mass religion. Let the professors of music sniffily declare a tune banal or sentimental; let the theologians loftily pronounce the words doggerel or even heretical, but if the people take that hymn to their hearts, sooner or later it will triumph.

Hymns plant spiritual time-bombs in the mind. One way or another, often as children, we learn hymns then as time wears on they slip our memories. But deep, deep in our minds, these magic images slumber on but can unaccountably come to life again, triggered by a crisis or the need to celebrate or the desire for comfort – and the detonator is the tune. Very often all we have to do is hum the tune and the words come back to us.

Some months ago, I read in the *Spectator* an extract from a letter written home by a First World War chaplain who was detailed to share the last hours of a British soldier who was to be shot at dawn for desertion in the face of the enemy. The soldier, said the chaplain, was a hard case, he listened stone-faced whilst the padre tried to get through to him the seriousness of his situation and to offer words of comfort. He tried reading passages from the Bible, saying well-known prayers, speaking pastorally to him. To no avail. Then as the sky began to lighten towards dawn, in sheer desperation the padre began to sing quietly some verses of well-known hymns. When he began 'Rock of Ages Cleft for Me' the soldier's face melted and he joined in the singing, knowing every word of a hymn he had sung at his mother's knee in the long-lost days of innocence. And they were able to speak urgently together of ultimate things.

It may be a blow to our *amour-propre* as preachers, but the chances are that a striking phrase from a hymn is more likely to lodge in someone's mind and be recalled when the crunch comes than any of our immaculately polished oratorical periods. Therefore hymns should always be chosen with great care, for they are the faith made portable, popular and persistent.

But back to the sermon: I recall as a theological student in the 1950s sitting on the platform of a packed Albert Hall in Manchester when a great Methodist preacher, the Rev. William Gowland, was at the height of his preaching powers. Because I was behind him, I could see only the back of his head as he preached but I found it possible to imagine his facial expressions by watching the congregation as it reacted to him. I saw his face in the people's eyes. At one point he must have frowned because they looked worried, then he obviously smiled because they relaxed as though anticipating a witticism. At another point he became stern and they leaned forward in their seats transfixed, almost fearing his next words.

So absorbed was the congregation in the sermon that all unconsciously it was acting as a mirror – reflecting and intensifying the preacher's passion. That's when I realized that preaching is a corporate act, something preacher and congregation do together. Indeed, Martin Luther claimed that there can be no Word of God without the People of God. Energizing your words as a preacher is all the power of corporate conviction, the assurance of a corporate faith and the impact of a corporate will.

Preacher and congregation are initially bound together not by anything the preacher says but by the mutual love and concern they feel for each other, grounded in their private prayers before they even meet. As it says in the first epistle of John: 'Everyone who loves is a child of God, but the unloving know nothing of God.' Where there is no such mutual caring, there is no revelation of God and therefore there can be no preaching. Only in an atmosphere permeated by love can God's voice be heard. This is one reason why Paul reacted so fiercely to quarrels in the early Church.

The interaction between preacher and congregation does not await the actual encounter in divine worship; it begins at the stage of sermon preparation when the preacher interrogates himself or herself in the presence of God, but the congregation has a lot of work to do if the sermon is to be effective. Its role in the preaching process is not simply to be an attentive listener. Indeed, it is worth asking oneself the question: apart from the natural nervousness evoked by any public occasion, what difference would it make to my sermon if I were to preach it in an empty church? It is possible to be so mechanically manuscript-bound that it is hard to see what impact the congregation could possibly make on the preaching process unless it nodded off or walked out in protest.

Some years ago, I was guest preacher at a rally which was held in an auditorium usually used as a theatre, with stage lighting. When it came to the time for the address the house lights were lowered so that the congregation was in darkness and I was illuminated by a spotlight. After five minutes I had to break off and ask for the house lights to be raised so that I could see the congregation's faces. Because I was robbed of eye-to-eye contact with them, my sermon was going to pieces.

This relationship between the preacher and congregation is dynamic. Thus, you may deliver the text of a sermon but they punctuate it, decisively affecting, for instance, the pace at which you develop your theme and the amount of time you are allowed to give to any part of it. In one sense, the sermon is a set of ideas on the march – and it is often the congregation that beats the drum and keeps the preacher moving.

In *The Reformed Pastor*, Richard Baxter writes, 'Look upon your congregation believingly, and with compassion.'[36] Have faith in the people, in their spiritual possibilities, in their capacity to rise to any challenge you may offer them, in their perennial optimism that you have something important to share with them. But also bear in mind, compassionately, their private preoccupations, worries and sorrows as you gauge the due weight of truth to lay upon them.

Another way of putting all this is to say that the sermon is a liturgical act. It is not a solo performance like a dramatic recitation in the middle of a musical programme. It is one element in a total experience, each part of which is important. In the end, the measure of a sermon is not what the preacher says but what the people do. The preacher utters but it is the congregation that preaches. You act upon the church in order that the church may act upon the world. Indeed, *as a preacher*, you have no access to the world except through the church, certainly not as a substitute for it.

The preacher confronts the Church with itself, the actual with the ideal, the seen with the unseen, *a* church with *the* Church. John Wesley advised his followers to preach Christ in all his offices as Prophet, Priest and King. It is patently obvious that such an undertaking is beyond the wit, intellect and dedication of any individual, however talented. The task belongs to the People of God because they are able to do together what none of them, including the preacher in the pulpit, could attempt in isolation. Wesley's dictum has its twentieth-century counterpart, a truism no doubt, but none the less true for that – only the whole Church can preach the whole Gospel to the whole World.

The preacher gathers up the experience of the People of God, measures it against the Gospel and articulates it. The preacher has spoken but it is the Church that has preached, and honesty compels one to admit that some of its sermons are pretty dreary. For the Church is made of the gritty stuff of the world; in fact, it *is* that bit of the shot through with the reconciling power of God.

Talking to his students about preaching, Dietrich Bonhoeffer the German theologian who was hanged in 1945 for plotting against Hitler said, 'I preach because the Church is there and I preach that the Church might be there. Church preaches to church.'[37]

In the last resort the preacher is at the mercy of the people, utterly vulnerable, doomed without their prayers and support. We preachers usually enter the sanctuary as the service begins as though from the outside, like guest stars on a light entertainment show. As the organ voluntary sinks and the choir take their places the preacher walks or is led into church. I'm torn about this practice. I can see that there is a powerful symbolic truth proclaimed here, that the people's salvation always comes to them from outside themselves. It is a lesson our proud, seemingly self-sufficient Western society needs to learn. We have the technical virtuosity to do virtually *anything* that is not self-evidently absurd – except one thing. We cannot save ourselves. Our salvation always comes from outside ourselves. Salvation doesn't well up like a great spring in our midst, it has to be brought to us. We cannot sit down with a wet towel round our heads and think our way to God; that truth breaks in from outside. Isn't that what incarnation means? The Tabernacle of God may dwell with men but it wasn't always so; there had to be a point at which history was cloven in two – the Word became flesh.

Hence, the preacher entering the sanctuary from outside it does remind the congregation that the Gospel has to be brought to them as it was to the first generation of Christians. And yet . . . in the end we preachers do not come *to* the congregation, we come *from* it. We are not aliens from another planet; we are fellow pew-dwellers of these people who in their wisdom or foolhardiness have commissioned us to speak to them. It is from them that I first heard the Gospel; they taught me the old, old story when I was a child, they nurtured me spiritually, tested my call to preach and gave me authority to do the work of a minister in the Church of God.

As preachers we speak not just *to* the people but *for* them and *with* them. It is a salutary experience to sit in the pews and share the worship of the congregation and its hearing of another preacher's word. Sadly, the ordained ministry get too few opportunities to do this. It's a pity, for the change in perspective can be startling. And it isn't just the natural curiosity of one preacher about the way another will deal with a subject or text. There is the psychic pressure of one's fellow pew-dwellers, all the invisible but real filaments that bind them together, or occasionally divide them. Because the Gospel consists of a finite number of facts we are bound to hear from another preacher, phrases, theological terms, biblical stories we employ ourselves and can mark how they are received in the body of the congregation. The preacher committed, in Bonhoeffer's words, to preaching from the Church to the church can learn much about the art of preaching from sitting in the midst of the congregation. It won't be codified knowledge but truth absorbed through the skin by observation and sensitivity.

Beware of succumbing to Nonconformity's traditional malaise and spend hours finding the exact words in which to couch the sermon whilst casually throwing together a few sentences to be directed at God in prayer. I have heard the parts of the service that precede the sermon described as 'the preliminaries'. If that is what the congregation has been schooled to think, then the preacher may as well save his breath. He is not confronting the People of God but an audience of sermon-tasters who think all they are required to do is to mark him out of ten.

We've already agreed that it is not the sermon alone which proclaims the Gospel. People used to travel very long distances to hear John Henry Newman say the Office, and C. H. Spurgeon's public reading of the Psalms was apparently a never-to-be-forgotten experience. The reverence with which Alexander Whyte opened the pulpit Bible to seek out his text, and at the end of the sermon, the decisive crash as he slammed it shut as though he had physically to tear himself away from it; these were not oratorical tricks, they were quite unconscious evidences of the centrality of the Word of God in his life.

One of the secrets of the power of Dr Leslie Weatherhead, minister of the City Temple, was the meticulous care with which every aspect of the service was planned – hymns, music, readings, pauses for reflection. One of his favourite texts was Moffatt's rendering of Philippians 4:8: 'Whatever is true or worthwhile or just or attractive or high-minded, keep on thinking about these things.' Every act of worship conducted by Weatherhead radiated just such a strong, positive, joyous emphasis on the worthiness of God in Christ. It was an uplifting atmosphere that lent wings to his sermons. He needed no perfervid oratory to flog the congregation into life.

A final comment about the relationship between the preacher and the congregation. The preacher, unlike the convicted felon, doesn't get time off for good conduct, or to put it differently there are no holiday Sundays in the pulpit. You must never declare a pact of mutual non-aggression with a congregation for any reason. By this I mean there is no state of spiritual equilibrium in which the congregation can remain suspended before, during and after the sermon. Once you preach and however you preach, you will change things, if only by undermining or reinforcing attitudes.

Some members of the congregation will have come to hear you in great expectancy or fear and may either be encouraged or let down by what they hear. It is one thing to be unable to fulfil their hopes in spite of your best efforts, quite another to disappoint them because you are at least homiletically taking a Sunday off.

Others in the congregation may be there purely by happenstance; they are neither conscious of great need nor harbouring particular hopes. Any one of the conventional reasons that impel people to come to church has brought them there. They may feel that the service has changed nothing because they arrive and leave in exactly the same state of genial spiritual neutrality, but from the preacher's point of view, a priceless opportunity may have been lost.

There is a point in the process of smelting when the metal is neither too hard nor too fluid to be shaped at will. But let the temperature drop or rise by a few degrees and nothing can be done with it, the whole operation must begin all over again. Similarly, the human personality undergoes strange fluxes. Sometimes we are sensitive, malleable, teachable; at other times we are hard, resistant, deaf to the voice of reason or even sanity. And on any given Sunday, quite unbeknown to you, someone in a congregation may be at such a point of maximum receptiveness. Though they've not necessarily asked for it, they would welcome bread and the preacher must not offer them a stone – even a very small, polished and painlessly swallowed pebble. The preacher can never safely assume there is such a thing as a dead Sunday because of bad weather or a poor congregation or an expectation that only the faithful will be in attendance and like the harvest sheaves they've already been safely gathered in. The uncertainty of life injects urgency into all our dealings, and especially those to do with God. That is at least one compelling reason why you cannot afford to take a vacation when you are in the pulpit.

If you are ever short of sermon illustrations, any of the volumes of rabbinical wisdom will furnish a fathomless treasure trove. One old rabbi was asked, 'Master, when ought we to make our peace with God?' He replied, 'Oh, not until one minute before you die.' 'But, Master,' the disciple protested, 'we don't know when we shall die!' 'Precisely,' said the rabbi. 'Do it now!'

P. T. Forsyth once told a congregation, 'When you reflect after worship, "What have I done today?" say to yourself, "I have done more than on any busiest part of the week, I have yielded myself to take part with the Church in Christ's finished act of redemption, which is greater than the making of the world."'[38] That is an awesome claim to make about the significance of Christian worship and your privileged part in it as a preacher.

As preachers we stand or fall by the Church, unless of course we fall outside it. In which case we can do what we like; in fact, that is all we can do, as we like. So we preach as best we can and run for cover in the Church which, having tested our call to preach, is prepared to accept the responsibility for our inadequacies, for our stumbling, halting words. Isaiah said, 'God has chosen to use people of stammering speech and an alien tongue to save his people.'

I began this discussion by warning you that preaching isn't difficult, it is downright impossible, but it embodies a goal that lures us on. Some words of Edward Shillito capture the challenge of the preacher's vocation. I hope you will feel able to echo them:

I who have given thee my best
Rejoice thy word is unexpressed,
And inexpressible must be
On this side of eternity;
And I with all my travail vast
Am glad that I must fail at last.

If I had found the Word complete
No glory could I march to meet
A pilgrim home from pilgrimage!
A soldier with no fight to wage!
But now my powers I still must spend
And go on failing to the end,
But failing I shall leave behind
Some hints of the Eternal mind,
And hungry pilgrims where I went
May find a broken sacrament.[39]

NOTES

1 *Introduction to The Call of God*, A. B. Davidson,
  Edinburgh, 1902
2 *The Craft of Sermon Construction*, W. E. Sangster,
  Epworth, 1949, p. 1
3 *The Art of Preaching*, C. Smyth, SPCK, 1940, p. 15
4 *The Myth of the Empty Church*, Robin Gill, SPCK,
  1993
5 Quoted in Craig, *Preaching in a Scientific Age*, SCM,
  1954, p. 13
6 Quoted in *Preachers I have Heard*, Gammie, Pickering
  and Inglis, n.d.
7 *Preaching from Camelot to Covenant*, McElvaney,
  Abingdon, 1989, p. 102
8 *Robertson of Brighton*, Henley Henson, Smith, Elder,
  1916, p. 49
9 Jeremiah 20:7 (AV)
10 Quoted in *The Art of Preaching*, Smith, Hodder, 1924,
   p. 202
11 Inscribed in Baker University, Kansas, of which Quayle
   was President
12 *Verbum Dei*, Horton, Fisher Unwin, 1893, p. 15
13 Title of a book by John V. Taylor published in 1972
14 *The Gospel and Authority*, Forsyth, Augsburg, 1972,
   pp. 24 et seq.

15 Ibid.
16 *Introduction to The Man Born to Be King*, Sayers, Gollancz, 1942
17 See *The Art of Preaching*, Smyth, SPCK, 1940
18 *Overhearing the Gospel*, Craddock, Abingdon, 1978, p. 13
19 Quoted in *In Christ's Stead*, Gossip, Hodder, 1925
20 Ibid.
21 *Early Christian Rhetoric*, Wilder, SCM, 1964
22 *The Quotable Chesterton*, Martin, Swan & Rabatin, Ignatius, 1986
23 Quoted by John Watson in *The Cure of Souls*, New York, 1897
24 Quoted by Gossip, ibid.
25 *The Quotable Chesterton*, ibid.
26 Smyth, ibid., p. 3
27 *Oh, What a Blow the Phantom Gave Me!* Carpenter, Paladin, 1976, p. 137
28 Source unknown
29 *Life of Alexander Whyte*, Barbour, Hodder, 1924, p. 236
30 Craddock, Ibid., p.66
31 *The Integrity of Preaching*, Knox, Epworth, 1957, pp. 42–3
32 *Obiter Scripta*, Maltby, Epworth, 1952
33 Watson, Ibid.
34 Source unknown
35 *Pew Rights,* Van Harn, Erdmans, 1992
36 *The Art of Preaching*, Smith, Hodder, 1924, p. 165
37 *Bonhoeffer*, Fant, Nelson, 1975, p. 138
38 Quoted by Professor A. M. Hunter in a lecture
39 *Obiter Scripta*, Maltby, Epworth, 1952, p. 100